Investment and Exit Decisions at the Plant Level

Contributions to Economics

Christoph M. Schneider
Research and Development Management: From the Soviet Union to Russia
1994. ISBN 3-7908-0757-5

Bernhard Böhm/Lionello F. Punzo (Eds.)
Economic Performance
1994. ISBN 3-7908-0811-3

Lars Olof Persson/Ulf Wiberg
Microregional Fragmentation
1995. ISBN 3-7908-0855-5

Ernesto Felli/Furio C. Rosati/Giovanni Tria (Eds.)
The Service Sector: Productivity and Growth
1995. ISBN 3-7908-0875-X

Giuseppe Munda
Multicriteria Evaluation in Fuzzy Environment
1995. ISBN 3-7908-0892-X

Giovanni Galizzi/Luciano Venturini (Eds.)
Economics of Innovation: The Case of Food Industry
1996. ISBN 3-7908-0911-X

David T. Johnson
Poverty, Inequality and Social Welfare in Australia
1996. ISBN 3-7908-0942-X

Rongxing Guo
Border-Regional Economics
1996. ISBN 3-7908-0943-8

Oliver Fratzscher
The Political Economy of Trade Integration
1996. ISBN 3-7908-0945-4

Ulrich Landwehr
Industrial Mobility and Public Policy
1996. ISBN 3-7908-0949-7

Arnold Picot/Ekkehard Schlicht (Eds.)
Firms, Markets, and Contracts
1996. Corr. 2nd printing 1997.
ISBN 3-7908-0947-0

Thorsten Wichmann
Agricultural Technical Progress and the Development of a Dual Economy
1997. ISBN 3-7908-0960-8

Ulrich Woitek
Business Cycles
1997. ISBN 3-7908-0997-7

Michael Carlberg
International Economic Growth
1997. ISBN 3-7908-0995-0

Massimo Filippini
Elements of the Swiss Market for Electricity
1997. ISBN 3-7908-0996-9

Giuseppe Gaburro (Ed.)
Ethics and Economics
1997. ISBN 3-7908-0986-1

Frank Hoster/Heinz Welsch/Christoph Böhringer
CO_2 Abatement and Economic Structural Change in the European Internal Market
1997. ISBN 3-7908-1020-7

Christian M. Hafner
Nonlinear Time Series Analysis with Applications to Foreign Exchange Rate Volatility
1997. ISBN 3-7908-1041-X

Sardar M. N. Islam
Mathematical Economics of Multi-Level Optimisation
1998. ISBN 3-7908-1050-9

Sven-Morten Mentzel
Real Exchange Rate Movements
1998. ISBN 3-7908-1081-9

Lei Delsen/Eelke de Jong (Eds.)
The German and Dutch Economies
1998. ISBN 3-7908-1064-9

Mark Weder
Business Cycle Models with Indeterminacy
1998. ISBN 3-7908-1078-9

Tor Rødseth (Ed.)
Models for Multispecies Management
1998. ISBN 3-7908-1001-0

Michael Carlberg
Intertemporal Macroeconomics
1998. ISBN 3-7908-1096-7

Sabine Spangenberg
The Institutionalised Transformation of the East German Economy
1998. ISBN 3-7908-1103-3

continued on page 187

Joachim Winter

Investment and Exit Decisions at the Plant Level

A Dynamic Programming Approach

With 5 Figures
and 20 Tables

Physica-Verlag
A Springer-Verlag Company

Series Editors
Werner A. Müller
Martina Bihn

Author
Dr. Joachim Winter
Sonderforschungsbereich 504
Universität Mannheim
D-68131 Mannheim, Germany

ISBN-13: 978-3-7908-1154-4 e-ISBN-13: 978-3-642-99803-4
DOI: 10.1007/978-3-642-99803-4

Cataloging-in-Publication Data applied for
Die Deutsche Bibliothek – CIP-Einheitsaufnahme
Winter, Joachim: Investment and exit decisions at the plant level: a dynamic programming approach; with 20 tables / Joachim Winter. – Heidelberg: Physica-Verl., 1998
(Contributions to economics)
ISBN-13: 978-3-7908-1154-4

Softcover Design: Erich Kirchner, Heidelberg

SPIN 10691829 88/2202-5 4 3 2 1 0 – Printed on acid-free paper

Fix it, sell it, or close it.

Jack F. Welch, CEO, General Electrics

Preface

This study was written while I was a doctoral student in the *Graduiertenkolleg Finanz- und Gütermärkte* at the University of Mannheim; it has been accepted as a doctoral dissertation in February 1997. I am indebted to my advisors, Professors Axel Börsch-Supan and Martin Hellwig at Mannheim and John Rust at Madison, for their encouragement and for many helpful discussions and comments.

At various stages, I benefited from comments on portions of the manuscript by, and from discussions with, Thomas Åstebro, Charles Calomiris, Timothy Dunne, Frank Gerhard, Annette Köhler, Jens Köke, Stephan Monissen, Gordon Phillips, Winfried Pohlmeier, Kenneth Troske, Wolfram Wissler and seminar participants at Columbia Business School, the University of Mannheim, the University of Tübingen, the University of Wisconsin at Madison, Yale University, the ENTER Jamborees at University College London, January 1995, and at Tilburg University, January 1997, at a Meeting of the *DFG-Schwerpunktprogramm Industrieökonomik und Inputmärkte*, Heidelberg, November 1996, and at the annual meeting of the *Verein für Socialpolitik*, Bern, September 1997. Silke Januszewski and Melanie Lührmann provided dedicated assistence during the preparation of the final version of the manuscript.

Parts of this research were conducted while I was visiting the Department of Economics at the University of Wisconsin at Madison during the 1996 Spring Semester. All computations involving confidential LRD data were performed while I was a research associate at the Center for Economic Studies, U.S. Bureau of the Census, Washington D.C., April–August 1996. I wish to thank both institutions for their hospitality; Timothy Dunne, Gordon Phillips, Arnold Reznek and Kenneth Troske for their invaluable help with the LRD database; and Steven Kaplan for allowing me to use (in Chapter 4) the financial status indicator variable he constructed with Luigi Zingales for a panel of U.S. firms. Financial support from *Deutsche Forschungsgemeinschaft* (through a scholarship and other resources provided by the *Graduiertenkolleg*) and from *Deutscher Akademischer Austauschdienst* is gratefully acknowledged.

Finally, I should like to thank Annette Köhler for all the support she gave me during the years I worked on this project, being far from her for quite some time.

Research results and conclusions expressed are those of the author and do not necessarily indicate concurrence by the U.S. Bureau of the Census or the Center for Economic Studies.

Contents

Chapter 1

Introduction

The empirical analysis of firms' investment decisions has experienced renewed interest during recent years, mainly driven by new developments in the theory of investment. This new literature addresses two related issues: First, the empirical failure of earlier neoclassical investment models in explaining stylized facts of firms' investment decisions, and second, the need to provide solid microfoundations for macroeconomic models in general. The resulting research program hence concentrates on models of firm investment which are both theoretically and empirically more satisfactory than the standard neoclassical framework. The ultimate goal is to better understand the dynamics of both disaggregate and aggregate investment in the presence of phenomena such as endogenous entry and exit decisions and non-standard constraints (irreversibilities, non-convex adjustment costs, or financial constraints). Hopefully, this research program will also result in a better understanding of the internal dynamics of the macroeconomy and its responses to exogenous shocks, be they real (technological) or nominal (monetary), in dynamic general equilibrium.

This study tries to make a small and very specific contribution to this research program: Its main purpose is to develop a flexible empirical framework that allows to test the implications of different aspects of the more recent investment literature. In particular, I will analyze a model of firms' intertemporal investment decisions that allows to incorporate various non-standard constraints, both on the "real" and on the "financial" sides of investment. This framework is built on the theory of Markov decision processes, a theory that can be used to develop very general models of economic decisions under uncertainty. At the same time, recent years have seen the development of many new econometric techniques for structural estimation of Markov decision processes. Such structural approaches have the advantage that they are not subject to the *Lucas critique* and hence allow for valid out-of-sample predictions and for the simulation of the effects of policy changes. Because of these theoretical and methodological advantages, it is conceivable that such a general framework will be useful in different fields of empirical investment research that might seem quite diverse on first sight.

New interest in the empirical analysis of firms' decisions has also been spurred (mostly in the U.S.) by the availability of new, comprehensive plant-level databases that facilitate the empirical analysis of investment models. For this reason, the second major aim of this study is to illustrate how the theoretical model can be used in actual empirical applications, stressing both the flexibility of this framework and the usefulness of plant-level data in the structural econometric analysis of investment decisions. In addition, such applications reveal that the main strength of the structual approach, the fact that it is firmly based on an intertemporal optimization problem, can become a problem in applied work: For successful estimation, a number of strong assumptions have to be made, and the researcher has to be very clear about these. It is my view, however, that the discipline required by structural modelling facilitates empirical work and, at the same time, makes it easier to compare and evaluate the results.

The remainder of this introduction discusses in more detail the issues that have just been sketched in order to motivate the choice of methods, empirical problems, and data.

Recent advances in the theory of firm investment

The neoclassical theory of firm investment has been extended along various dimensions in recent years. In an attempt to classify these developments, one could isolate three major areas on which research efforts have concentrated: the "real" side of an individual firm's investment decision, the role of financial markets in funding real investment, and the importance of market interactions for firms' investment behavior.

The first area focuses on theoretical models of individual firms' investment decisions and on empirical tests of these models. Generally, the empirical performance of standard intertemporal optimization models of investment is unsatisfactory. More recent investment models therefore stress various forms of non-standard constraints, such as irreversibilities or non-convex capital stock adjustment costs, and generally allow for a more explicit role of uncertainty. This approach reveals that there is an "option value of waiting" associated with firms' investment decisions. Another important development in the empirical analysis of investment is the use of plant-level data which helps to reduce aggregation biases.

In addition to non-standard constraints on investment, there is a related second area that attracted much interest recently – the role of imperfect markets, in particular, imperfectly competitive output markets. These models are relevant for the analysis of investment decisions because they generate endogenous exit rules that allow to explain frequently observed firm or plant exits. One of the apparent successes of the recent theoretical investment literature is that these models can explain some stylized facts both of individual firms' investment behavior and of aggregate investment that were difficult to rationalize with earlier neoclassical models. However, direct empirical tests of these models are still quite rare because firms' optimal policies are typically non-linear (e. g., they may involve discrete choices). Hence, they are difficult to handle in econometric studies.

The third area of research concentrates on the effects of financial constraints on firm investment, credit rationing being a leading example. Such effects are relevant for economic policy on different levels of aggregation. At the level of the individual firm or industry, financial constraints (mainly thought to be caused by imperfect information about firm characteristics on the side of the lender) might influence firm growth and survival: Because of financial constraints, firms that have promising innovations at hand may be prevented from undertaking R&D or investment. Once they have started an investment project or have entered a market with a new product, they may still be driven out because of a lack of funds. Both effects are not desirable from a welfare view. Also at the industry level, the provision of outside finance has been identified as one of the major forces in industrial restructuring, for example, by driving inefficient firms out of the market or by preventing firms from undertaking projects with low expected returns. In this sense, financial constraints can have a positive welfare effect. Finally, from a macroeconomic view, financial constraints might explain the propagation of nominal shocks through the economy (via the "lending" or "credit channel" of monetary policy). All these models, however, assume that the provision of outside finance actually affects firms' investment decisions. Trivial as this might seem, hard empirical evidence is difficult to obtain because of various conceptual and measurement problems. Not surprisingly, the available evidence on the role of financial constraints is mixed.

Two of these areas of current investment research, non-standard constraints and financial constraints, form the background for this study while the influence of market interactions is reflected in endogenous exit rules that extend the investment model. The related literature is briefly reviewed in Chapter 2.

A theoretical model of firm behavior

The theoretical model of firm behavior that I sketch in this study is based on a very general theory of intertemporal decisions under uncertainty, the theory of Markov decision processes. In such models, dynamic programming methods are used to characterize economic agents' (here, firms') optimal policies conditional on a specified set of state variables whose dynamic evolution is at least partially controlled by the agents' decisions. In a model of firm investment, the decision variables include (at least) investment, and the related state variable is the firm's capital stock.

While the Markov decision process approach allows for both continuous and discrete control variables, and standard models take investment as a continuous variable, the framework suggested here interprets firms' decisions as a mixed discrete-continuous Markov decision problem. Exit is modelled as a second (discrete) choice available to the firm. This approach allows to incorporate various non-standard constraints. After discretizing the continuous control variable, the mixed discrete-continuous model can be solved by standard dynamic programming techniques. Also, the resulting dynamic discrete-choice model is amenable to structural econometric estimation using maximum likelihood methods.

The most important aspect of the empirical model of firm behavior developed here is that it comprises not only intertemporal investment decisions but also endogenous market exit decisions. From a methodological point of view, this allows to control consistently for selection (survival) effects in a structural model. While conceptually straightforward, this approach has rarely been used in empirical studies. Note also that the exit choice is naturally modelled as a discrete decision, so the dynamic discrete-choice framework seems fairly reasonable for models with endogenous exit.

Econometric techniques for structural estimation of dynamic models of investment are still being developed. For discrete decision processes, one direction of research concentrates on nested numerical solution algorithms, and I follow this approach here. In particular, I use a variant of Rust's (1987, 1988) nested fixed-point algorithm. Basically, the idea is to derive the optimal solution of the dynamic control problem numerically in an inner loop, for given parameter values. This might involve the use of advanced simulation techniques when choices take only discrete values. Then the parameter values themselves can be estimated in an outer loop using standard maximum likelihood routines. There are, of course, other methods for structural estimation of dynamic optimization problems, and it has not yet been resolved which one – if any – is to be preferred. The empirical results of this study, however, suggest that the nested fixed-point algorithm works well for the dynamic model of firm decisions developed here.

Plant-level investment and firm-level financial constraints

The empirical study presented in Chapter 4 analyzes the effects of financial constraints on firm investment. As mentioned earlier, this issue has received much interest in both the financial economics and macroeconomics literatures: Finding such effects would be evidence in favor of "credit channel" theories of monetary policy transmission. It would help to understand the role of financial institutions in the restructuring of industries, and it would provide advice for designing policies that help small, innovative businesses to survive. Relative to the extensive empirical literature on this issue, the empirical approach used here tries to address three remaining conceptual problems. First, I account for exogenous exit decisions; second, I use plant level data to reduce aggregation biases, and third, I use a new indicator variable for identifying financially constrained firms. I will sketch the relevance of these issues in turn.

The mixed discrete-continuous model of firm behavior presented in Section 3.3.1, reflecting joint investment and exit decisions, can be extended to allow for (possibly) imperfect capital markets. In particular, the aim is to assess whether financial constraints affect firms' investment and market exit decisions. As noted above, ignoring endogenous exits introduces selection biases to empirical investment models, and these might be important when the probability of exit depends on the firm's financial situation.

In Section 2.1.4, I argue that using firm-level data instead of data recorded at the individual project or plant level might introduce aggregation biases to empirical models of investment decisions. An extensive research program, using a comprehensive U.S. plant-level database (the Longitudinal Research Database, described in Section 4.A.1), has shown that the dynamics of output, investment and labor demand are much richer at the plant level than firm-level data would suggest; see, *inter alia*, the seminal work by Davis *et al.* (1996). It is therefore likely that the effects of financial constraints are most severe at the plant level and at least partially washed out when investment is aggregated to the firm level. In the empirical part of this study, I therefore combine firm-level data on firms' financial status with plant-level data on "real" investment decisions.

The financial status indicator used to identify financially constrained firms has only recently been constructed by Kaplan and Zingales (1997), and while the sample covered is fairly small and definitive conclusions are therefore difficult, the results of this study indicate that the new indicator helps explain investment and exit decisions at the plant level (after controlling for expected profitability in a structural model). At a minimum, this result adds another piece of empirical evidence to the view that a firm's financial situation affects its investment (and also market exit) decisions. The structural approach used for estimating the dynamic model of investment and exit decisions under financial constraints also allows to conduct valid policy simulations, and an example is given at the end of Chapter 4.

A note on methodology

Throughout this study, I adopt the view that firms' decisions are profit-maximizing and rational. In particular, I assume that investment and market exit decisions are the solution to an intertemporal optimization problem under rational expectations. This is a maintained assumption throughout the study, and I will mention alternative views of firm decisions, and of economic behavior in general, only in passing. As discussed in detail in Chapter 3, the assumption of rational maximizing behavior has no empirical content *per se*. To give the intertemporal optimization framework empirical content, further (structural) assumptions have to be imposed on the form of agents' preferences or technologies and on their beliefs about future state variables. When such models are estimated structurally, it is possible to test these assumptions, but any test will be jointly for the maintained assumption of rational maximizing behavior and the particular structural assumptions made.

Overview of the study

The remainder of this study is structured as follows. In Chapter 2, I review the theoretical and empirical literature on investment decisions with special reference to non-standard and financial constraints, and I sketch a research program for the structural empirical analysis of firm behavior. The theoretical model of firms' joint investment and exit decisions is presented in Chapter 3, together with reviews of Markov decision processes in general and of approaches for their econometric estimation. In Chapter 4, I present an empirical application of this framework, the analysis of firms' investment and market exit decisions under financial constraints. Chapter 5 contains some concluding remarks.

Chapter 2

Theory and empirics of investment: a selective review of the literature

This chapter contains a review of the literature which forms the background for the empirical study presented in Chapter 4. I concentrate on the two major areas of recent research on firms' investment decisions identified in the introduction: Recent developments in formulating and estimating models of firms' "real" investment decisions (Section 2.1), and financial constraints that may affect firms' investment (Section 2.2). As discussed in the introduction, the first area has recently experienced major theoretical advances which have not yet entered empirical practice, while in the second area, there has been much empirical research in the last decade, with many of the theoretical advances in the first literature having been largely ignored so far.

The review of theoretical investment models in this chapter is intentionally selective. However, I address two aspects which are more relevant for economic policy than the theoretical models themselves. These are, first, macroeconomic implications of non-standard investment models and of financial constraints, and second, empirical tests of these models. The main conclusion is that while there have been major advances in the theory of investment (with respect to both real and financial aspects), the empirical evidence is mixed, and many theoretical insights have never really been translated into structural econometric models. Their implications, however, are generally judged to be compatible with empirical stylized facts.

The chapter ends with some remarks on the structural empirical analysis of investment models. The aim of the research program outlined in Section 2.3 is to provide an (admittedly stylized) model of firms' investment decisions that can be extended by various non-standard constraints (in particular, non-convex adjustment costs, irreversibilities, and financial constraints), and which is amenable to structural econometric estimation.

2.1 Theories of firm investment and their empirical performance

In this section, I review traditional and more recent models of firm investment behavior, with special emphasis on their empirical performance. I begin with a simple version of the standard "neoclassical" model of firms' investment decisions and discuss how reduced-form and structural econometric specifications can be derived (Section 2.1.1).[1] The remainder of this section focuses on recent developments in the investment literature that address some of the empirical failures of the neoclassical model: Section 2.1.2 concentrates on non-standard constraints such as uncertainty, non-convex adjustment costs and irreversibilities in a single-firm (decision theoretic) framework. In Section 2.1.3, I analyze the effects of market interactions on investment behavior in models with imperfect competition. Finally, I discuss the role of aggregation bias and the use of plant-level data in empirical investment studies in Section 2.1.4.

2.1.1 The neoclassical model of firm investment

Neoclassical models of firm investment can be classified in two groups (see Blundell *et al.* (1996)): The first group consists of models which derive the optimal capital stock from the firm's maximization problem but do not explicitly consider the adjustment process when capital is not at its optimal level. These models are associated mainly with the name of Dale Jorgenson (1963, 1967, 1971). Most empirical studies of investment in the 1960s and 1970s have been based on these models, and dynamics were introduced exogenously by imposing lag structures. I do not discuss these earlier models in detail here; the monograph by Nickell (1978) reviews both theory and empirics of these models.

---

[1] I will discuss the econometric estimation of reduced-form vs. structural models in more detail in Section 3.2.

The second group of neoclassical investment models characterize the complete evolution of the firm's capital stock resulting from the underlying optimization problem. They are based on work by, *inter alia*, Eisner and Strotz (1963), Gould (1968), Treadway (1969), and Lucas and Prescott (1971); a textbook treatment can be found in Sargent (1987b), Chapter 14. The firm's optimal investment policy as derived from an intertemporal optimization problem can be characterized in two ways: First, in terms of Tobin's q, and second, by an Euler equation (both concepts will be defined shortly). Essentially, both concepts are based on optimality conditions that equate (expected) marginal costs and benefits of an additional unit of capital in the presence of some adjustment cost. They differ, however, in the way in which they treat expectations, an issue to which I return below. Both conditions have also been used to formulate econometric models of firm investment.

Next, I derive Tobin's q and an Euler equation from a simple intertemporal optimization model of firm investment; the presentation here follows Blundell *et al.* (1996). Then I discuss the empirical performance of these two implementations of the intertemporal optimality condition for firm investment.

The firm's intertemporal optimization problem

In the standard neoclassical model of investment, the firm is assumed to maximize, in the planning period $t = 0$, the expected present value of net cash flows[2] given by

$$V_0 = E\left[\sum_{t=0}^{\infty}(1+r)^{-t}\Pi_t\right], \tag{2.1}$$

where r is the interest rate, here assumed to be constant for simplicity[3], and Π_t is the net cash flow in period t. The firm's decision variables are current investment, i_t, and variable inputs, given by the vector l_t (which can be thought of as consisting just of labor, for simplicity). These

[2] Note that maximizing the expected value of cash flows is equivalent to maximizing the expected present value of (dividend) payments to the firm's shareholders if asset markets are (strongly) efficient.

[3] See Blundell *et al.* (1996) for a version of the model with time-varying interest rates.

decision variables enter the optimization problem via the firm's cash flow given by

$$\begin{aligned} \Pi_t &= \Pi(k_t, l_t, i_t) \\ &= p_t \left[f(k_t, l_t) - c(k_t, i_t) \right] - p_t^l l_t - p_t^k i_t \,. \end{aligned} \tag{2.2}$$

It is further assumed that the firm uses a single capital good k_t which is the only quasi-fixed factor of production. All other inputs can be adjusted instantaneously and costlessly. The production function is denoted by $f(k_t, l_t)$, the adjustment cost function is given by $c(k_t, i_t)$, and p_t, p_t^k and p_t^l are the prices of output, the capital good and other factors, respectively. Finally, the firm's capital stock evolves over time according to the recursion,

$$k_t = (1 - \delta) k_{t-1} + i_t \,, \tag{2.3}$$

where δ is the (physical) rate of capital depreciation.

Before deriving the solution to the firm's optimization problem, a few assumptions of the neoclassical model are worth being noted. The adjustment cost function is assumed to be strictly convex in investment, and investment is assumed to be fully reversible; the consequences of relaxing these assumptions are discussed in Section 2.1.2. Product and factor markets are assumed to be competitive, hence the firm is a price taker for both inputs and outputs. The implications of imperfect competition on output markets are the subject of Section 2.1.3.

The solution to the maximization problem (2.1) subject to (2.3) can be obtained by using dynamic programming methods (discussed in detail in Section 3.1 below). For the purpose of this introduction, I am not interested in technical details, so I focus directly on the first-order conditions for capital investment,

$$0 = \frac{\partial \Pi_t}{\partial k_t} + \frac{\partial \Pi_t}{\partial i_t} + E\left[(1+r) \frac{\partial V_{t+1}}{\partial k_t} \right] \quad \text{and} \tag{2.4}$$

$$\frac{\partial V_t}{\partial k_{t-1}} = (1 - \delta) \frac{\partial \Pi_t}{\partial k_t} + (1 - \delta) E\left[(1+r) \frac{\partial V_{t+1}}{\partial k_t} \right] , \tag{2.5}$$

and for the variable inputs,

$$0 = \frac{\partial \Pi_t}{\partial l_t} \,. \tag{2.6}$$

Because variable inputs are assumed to be adjusted instantaneously according to (2.6), they are typically suppressed in intertemporal investment models. It should, however, be noted that the (optimal) levels of variable factors, determined given the capital stock in place, yield the firm's current output and gross revenue via the production function.

Focusing on the investment decision, the two first-order conditions for capital investment can be combined to yield

$$\frac{\partial V_t}{\partial k_{t-1}} = -(1-\delta)\frac{\partial \Pi_t}{\partial i_{t-1}} . \tag{2.7}$$

The left-hand side represents the change in firm value if the capital stock were increased by one unit in the last period, while the right-hand side is the cost of installing one unit of additional capital. Condition (2.7) is a standard optimality condition, equating marginal benefits and marginal costs.

This optimality condition, however, involves an unobservable quantity, the shadow value of capital given by $\partial V_t/\partial k_{t-1}$. For empirical studies, the shadow value of capital has to be approximated by observable quantities, and this can been done in two different ways. First, one can try to approximate the shadow value of capital in (2.7). This yields an expression known as Tobin's q. Second, one can exploit the so-called Euler equation (2.5). For both approaches, certain assumptions about the nature of adjustment costs and expectation formation have to be made. I present these approaches in turn.

Optimal investment policies: Tobin's q

Exploiting the fact that the firm is a price taker in all markets, (2.2) can be used to write

$$\frac{\partial \Pi_t}{\partial i_t} = -p_t\frac{\partial c_t}{\partial i_t} - p_t^k \quad \text{and} \tag{2.8}$$

$$\frac{\partial \Pi_t}{\partial k_t} = p_t\left[\frac{\partial f_t}{\partial k_t} - \frac{\partial c_t}{\partial k_t}\right] . \tag{2.9}$$

Using these expressions together with (2.7) gives

$$\begin{aligned}\frac{\partial c_t}{\partial i_t} &= \frac{p_t^k}{p_t}\left[\frac{\frac{\partial V_t}{\partial k_{t-1}}\frac{1}{1-\delta}}{p_t^k} - 1\right] \\ &= \frac{p_t^k}{p_t}\left[q_t - 1\right] .\end{aligned} \tag{2.10}$$

Here, the expression $(\frac{\partial V_t}{\partial k_{t-1}}\frac{1}{1-\delta})/p_t^k$ is Tobin's marginal q, the ratio of the shadow value of one unit of capital and the price of an additional unit of capital. In the absence of adjustment costs, the capital stock is chosen such that q_t equals unity.[4] With adjustment costs, the level of investment is an increasing function of the deviation of q_t from unity.

For an econometric application, further assumptions are required. First, functional forms for the production adjustment cost functions have to be chosen, and second, an approximation for the shadow value of capital that enters q has to be found. Typically, adjustment costs are assumed to be quadratic (e. g., Summers (1981)). If one assumes that the production function $f(k_t, l_t)$ and the adjustment cost function $c(l_t, i_t)$ are linear-homogeneous in their arguments (i. e., that there are constant returns to scale), the unobserved shadow value of capital can be replaced by the *average* value of existing capital (Hayashi (1982)). With these assumptions, an empirically tractable version of the q-model given by (2.10) can be derived. After some manipulation, one obtains an investment equation that depends just on observable quantities:

$$\begin{aligned} \frac{i_t}{k_t} &= \alpha_0 + \alpha_1 \left[\frac{V_t}{(1-\delta) p_t^k k_{t-1}} - 1 \right] \frac{p_t^k}{p_t} \\ &= \alpha_0 + \alpha_1 \tilde{q}_t \, , \end{aligned} \tag{2.11}$$

where $\tilde{q}_t$ denotes *average* (rather than marginal) q, and α_0 and α_1 are constants. All expectations enter the investment function only via (average) $\tilde{q}_t$ which in turn reflects the forward-looking stock-market valuation of the firm's capital stock. Note that this investment equation is a reduced form of the underlying intertemporal optimization model of firm's investment decisions.

The validity of standard reduced-form models of firm investment has been questioned by many studies in recent years.[5] Generally speaking, traditional models of corporate investment such as the earlier neoclassical approach pioneered by Jorgenson or more recent reduced-form models based on Tobin's q have had only limited success in describing firm behavior. A major deficiency of such reduced-form approaches is that in theory, it is marginal q which determines investment; observable to the empirical economist, however, is only average $\tilde{q}$ (say, from accounting

---

[4] This condition is equivalent to the one obtained from Jorgenson's more traditional investment model; see Abel (1980).

[5] Chirinko (1993) provides a comprehensive overview of the empirical investment literature.

data). As discussed before, rather strong assumptions are necessary concerning the measurement of the shadow value of capital to make the model empirically tractable. Even in a quite sophisticated attempt to explain investment in a q-theory framework, Abel and Blanchard (1986) found that the data do not support the basic restrictions implied by the q-theory. Whited (1994) provides a detailed analysis of the empirical failure of the q-theory framework to identify adjustment costs.

Structural estimation of Euler equation models

An alternative to reduced-form approaches are structural models of investment, i. e., models that are derived directly from the intertemporal optimization problem. These models exploit the Euler equation (2.5); an early example for this approach is Abel (1980). This approach is more complicated than the simple intertemporal model presented here suggests, because expectations have to be treated explicitly (i. e., a rational expectations assumption is invoked). I do not discuss this approach in detail here; a more general discussion of structural econometric methods that are based on Euler equations can be found in Section 3.1.2. One of the main conceptual advantages of these structural approaches is that they do not rely on Tobin's q and hence are not affected by its mismeasurement. While structural models of the type discussed here are widely believed to be superior to reduced-form models for theoretical reasons, their empirical performance is mixed. This apparent failure is partly attributed to the statistical properties of the econometric estimators that are used to estimate Euler equations, the so-called generalized method of moments (GMM) estimators.

Oliner *et al.* (1995) compare the forecasting performance of traditional reduced-form models of investment (among others, a Jorgenson-type neoclassical and a q-theory model) with two Euler equation specifications. They conclude that "the Euler equations produce extremely poor forecasts of investment" (p. 807) and, judged by their out-of-sample forecasting performance, are dominated by traditional models. In addition to the poor finite-sample properties of GMM estimators, they cite the fact that the standard Euler equation approach does not account for irreversible investment and non-convex adjustment costs as potential reasons for the poor performance of structural Euler equation investment models.

In a similar study, Fuhrer *et al.* (1995) also find poor performance of Euler equation based GMM estimators when compared with maximum likelihood (ML) estimators of a linear-quadratic inventory model. Fuhrer *et al.* use firm-level data from nondurables manufacturing as well as Monte Carlo experiments to evaluate both methods. They conclude: "Data-based GMM estimates ... vary widely, generally rejecting the model. Monte Carlo experiments reveal that the GMM estimates are often biased (apparently due to poor instruments), statistically insignificant, economically implausible, and dynamically unstable. The ML estimates are generally unbiased (even in misspecified models), statistically significant, economically plausible, and dynamically stable." (p. 115)

2.1.2 Recent developments in the investment literature

Based on the empirical studies presented, it can be said that traditional models of firms' investment decisions, both based on q-theory approaches and on Euler equations, have had only limited success in describing firm behavior as observed in the data. For example, one of the central empirical stylized facts about firm behavior is that "businesses change their demand more slowly than the shocks to input demand warrant" (Hamermesh and Pfann (1996), p. 1264). This is particularly true for firm investment, where it has long been recognized that capital stocks change slowly over time. It is the aim of this section to identify economic mechanisms that have been developed in the theoretical literature to explain slow or lumpy adjustment of firms' capital stocks and to see how they have been, or could be, tested empirically. Of the many aspects that have been considered in this new literature, I concentrate on three issues that are, arguably, of particular empirical relevance: a closer analysis of the role of uncertainty, non-convex adjustment costs, and irreversibilities in investment decisions. Below, I take up these issues in turn.

Let me first sketch the central idea of this new variety of investment models (which use techniques developed by financial economists in the theory of option pricing). Once one takes into account the fact that investment is subject to some kind of non-standard constraint (such as non-convex adjustment costs or irreversibilities), the timing of investment decisions matters, and waiting has a positive value, the *option value of waiting*, a term dating back to McDonald and Siegel (1986): Postponing investment decisions allows to gather more information about the expected profits of a project. Hence, an investment project that is available to the firm can be regarded as a financial call option as long as it has not been started (or, exercised, as the term for a financial option would be). Correspondingly, once a project has been started, the firm will continuously monitor its success, the continuation decision taking the form of an optimal stopping rule.

Despite the recent investment literature's wealth of interesting theoretical results, empirical evidence is still sparse. The main reason for this lack of empirical work is that most recent investment models use sophisticated intertemporal optimization frameworks to derive optimal investment policies. While in general, optimal policies can be interpreted as *reduced forms* in an econometric context, they often involve unobservable quantities such as risk or uncertainty which are difficult to handle empirically. Usually, some kind of proxy variable has to be used to measure these quantities, which might prove unsatisfactory in practice. At the same time, structural estimation of intertemporal optimization models is generally not a simple task and requires a host of auxiliary assumptions. In many cases, it is not clear whether the results of a structural estimation exercise are robust with respect to these assumptions. It is one of the central aims of this study to provide an intertemporal optimization framework for the analyis of firm investment that might eventually allow to test some of the models discussed in this section in a consistent framework; this is the subject of Chapter 3. In the remainder of this section, I present exisiting evidence on the recent investment literature.

Uncertainty

Economists are only beginning to exploit the analogy of real and financial investments, yet some interesting results have already been derived. For example, as these models stress the relevance of uncertainty for investment decisions, interest rates are no longer the crucial determinant of corporate investment. It is risk that matters (i. e., both risk intrinsic to a particular project and overall uncertainty about the prospects of an economy). This result might help to explain why empirically, aggregate investment is by far not as responsive to changes in real interest rates as standard models would suggest. A comprehensive overview of this literature can be found in Dixit and Pindyck (1994); see also Caballero and Pindyck (1996). Abel *et al.* (1996), for example, use an option-value framework to analyze the effect of uncertainty on investment: "Generally, the option to expand reduces the incentive [to invest], while the option to to divest raises it" (p. 753). This paper is particularly interesting because it links the option-value approach to the more traditional q-theory framework of investment decisions.

There are few studies that explicitly analyze the relationship between investment and uncertainty, and the results are far from conclusive; see Leahy and Whited (1996) for a recent overview. As most of the recent literature on investment analyzes the effects of uncertainty jointly with other aspects such as irreversibility or non-convex adjustment costs, the effects of uncertainty are difficult to separate from other aspects of the empirical model of investment (I will discuss some of these studies below). Leahy and Whited (1996) develop a more direct approach that allows to test the relationship between uncertainty and investment using firm-level data. Essentially, they estimate reduced-form relationships between investment and uncertainty. The measure they use for the uncertainty faced by the firm is based on standard CAPM arguments; in particular, they focus on the variance of the firm's daily stock returns for each year in the sample.[6] Their central result is that "an increase in uncertainty decreases investment, primarily through its effect on [Tobin's marginal] q" (p. 77). In a second step, they employ sample-split criteria to test the relative importance of alternative theories of investment, judging that irreversible investment is "the most likely explanation for the observed correlation between investment and uncertainty" (*ibid.*).

Non-convex adjustment costs

Adjustment costs play an important role even in simple investment models (such as the neoclassical model presented in Section 2.1.1) because they ensure the existence of a well-defined investment function. Looking closer at adjustment costs, an important distinction is that of gross vs. net adjustment of the capital stock of which, in turn, capital stock adjustment costs are assumed to be a function. The general form of an adjustment cost function used earlier, $c(k_t, i_t)$, allows for both aspects.

---

[6] Leahy and Whited go some way to derive an *ex ante* measure of uncertainty based on option prices rather than stock prices, carefully constructing volatility forecasts using vector autoregression techniques.

Hamermesh and Pfann (1996) note that the concept used in most of the existing literature is that of gross adjustment costs, a fact that they attribute, at least partially, to the relatively poor quality of capital stock data (while investment can be better measured).[7]

The assumption used in standard models of investment is that the capital stock adjustment cost function is convex, more specifically, that adjustment costs are a quadratic function of the (gross or net) change in the capital stock. As discussed by Hamermesh and Pfann (1996), there are at least three alternative functional forms for adjustment costs that have been proposed in the literature, and while the quadratic case has the virtue of being easy to handle in theoretical models, "simply imposing [it], no matter how many times it has been done, in no way speaks to the correctness of the underlying assumption" (p. 1271).

Here, I concentrate on the case of "lumpy" adjustment costs and discuss both their theoretical implications and the available empirical evidence. For a detailed discussion of the other two main alternatives to quadratic adjustment costs, asymmetric convex costs and piecewise linear costs, see the survey by Hamermesh and Pfann (1996). Important contributions to this literature are, *inter alia*, Bertola and Caballero (1990) and Caballero and Engel (1994) who consider so-called (s, S) investment policies. These policies are well-known from optimization models with adjustment costs, where (s, S) denote endogenously determined (i. e., state-dependent) threshold values for taking some sort of action (such as investment). Caballero and Leahy (1996) discuss how fixed costs of investment affect the standard q-theory framework, effectively destroying its empirical content.

Caballero *et al.* (1997) analyze the dynamics of employment flows over the business cycle. Building on their earlier, primarily theoretical work, they use plant-level data taken from the Longitudinal Research Database (LRD)[8] to estimate a dynamic model of desired employment to explore

[7] Also, when economists consider adjustment costs for capital, they usually think of *internal* costs of adjusting the capital stock to its desired level. Another concept of adjustment costs is that of *external* costs introduced by Witte (1963). According to this concept, adjustment costs arise because the supply of capital goods is assumed to be inelastic.

[8] For details on the LRD and on the role of plant-level data in empirical investment models, see Section 4.A.1.

firms' labor input adjustment process. Their main findings for firm-level adjustment indicate that there are both important non-linearities in adjustment technologies and non-convexities in adjustment costs. These results allow the authors to derive aggregate employment dynamics which are firmly based on observed (microeconomic) behavior of firms. Caballero *et al.* note that (for technical reasons related to their estimation procedure) they had to restrict their analysis to firms which operated continuously in the 1972–80 sample period. They are well aware that this introduces some selection bias since small firms (with less than 250 employees) are not contained in their data, and because exits are ignored.[9]

Cooper *et al.* (1995) investigate cyclical investment fluctuations that are due to discrete changes in plants' stocks of capital. Their analysis is based on the assumption of non-convex adjustment costs for capital (in particular, small adjustments of the capital stock are assumed either not feasible or undesirable). The authors construct a stochastic model of machine replacement and simulate adjustment dynamics. They are also interested in the connection between the timing of large investment episodes at the plant level and fluctations in aggregate investment. Finally, they test some implications of their model using LRD data and a hazard-function approach.[10] The sample used for estimation is restricted to 6,900 large plants which are continuously operating in the estimation period (1972–91). The authors state that "entry and exit are obviously of interest" (p. 16) in the context of their study, but they choose not to deal with it explicitly (as their empirical model is already quite involved). The main finding is that plants do not invest very frequently and, over time, they tend to concentrate a large portion of their investment in shorter intervals. Similar findings have been obtained by Isgut (1997) using data for 2,000 manufacturing plants from Columbia.

---

[9] I will discuss selection biases caused by ignoring endogenous exits in models of firm behavior below.

[10] Cooper *et al.* also discuss the possibility of estimating a model with non-convex adjustment costs using structural methods like Rust's nested fixed-point algorithm (the method used in this study, see Section 3.2.3).

Irreversibility

As in the case of non-convex adjustment costs, irreversibilities are important for macroeconomic phenomena as well. Bertola and Caballero (1994), for example, analyze the effects of firm-level irreversibilities for aggregate investment in an (s, S) framework.

The central idea of the literature on irreversibilities is that there is a wedge between the prices paid for new capital goods and those received when selling used capital goods. This theory, therefore, can be tested on different levels. First, one can test whether such a wedge actually exists, and second, the theoretical implications of irreversibility can be tested themselves. An early attempt to estimate the resale and salvage values of machinery and equipment is Hulten and Wykoff (1981); a more recent example for this approach is Asplund (1995). He analyzes the valuation of metalworking machinery in Swedish manufacturing industries over the 1960–90 period. His main finding is that for an average "new" machine, firms can expect to get back only 10–55 % of the initial price. He attributes this fact largely to the high fixed costs in buying and selling used capital, causing second-hand markets to work poorly. These empirical findings are roughly in line with the arguments used in the theoretical literature to motivate the existence of irreversibilities (see, e. g., Dixit and Pindyck (1994), p. 8).[11]

Concerning the second approach, there is as yet not much direct empirical support for the role of irreversibility in investment decisions. Dixit and Pindyck (1994), pp. 423–425, discuss the sparse evidence available so far, judging that the lack of empirical support should be viewed as "an opportunity and challenge" (p. 425). There are basically two ways of testing the theory of investment under uncertainty with irreversibilities (or non-convex adjustment costs, for that matter): Structural approaches based on a full optimization problem with some non-standard constraint, and indirect (i. e., reduced-form) approaches that focus on some implication of an investment model, using only observed outcomes but no structural assumptions.

---

[11] Similar arguments are used by Shleifer and Vishny (1992) in their analysis of liquidation values and optimal capital structure; their main interest, however, is the role of asset liquidation values in takeovers or divestures and the influence of business cycle variations in the ability to sell off firms' assets. They also provide some casual evidence on these issues.

There are some studies that use the indirect approach, i. e., that test some implications of models of irreversible investment. One example is a paper by Pindyck and Solimano (1993). In particular, they concentrate on the "hurdle", or threshold, rates of return required for projects to be undertaken; theory suggests that these should be quite high compared to standard models. Pindyck and Solimano find some empirical support, but as Eberly (1993) points out in a comment to that paper, they have to construct several proxy variables because the hurdle rate itself is unobservable.

Dixit and Pindyck (1994) note that structural estimation of investment models, based on the optimality conditions of a full stochastic dynamic programming model, is a promising approach (p. 424). The structural approach is also the one taken in this study. In particular, I focus on market exit rules derived from a structural investment model. The idea is that firms make, in addition to the investment decision (which is subject to some potentially severe measurement problems), a second decision, to remain in the market or to exit. The exit decision is both firmly based on the underlying optimization problem (through an optimal stopping rule), and relatively easily observable in microdata (at least in principle, as most firm panels contain observed exits). However, this opens up many new issues. The role of endogenous exit decisions in theoretical and empirical studies of firms' investment behavior is discussed in the next section.

2.1.3 Endogenous market structure, entry and exit, and investment

The previous section focused on the analysis of "pure" investment decisions in the recent literature. Here, I concentrate on two other aspects that have received some interest recently: The endogeneity of the market structure in imperfectly competitive markets, in particular, the endogeneity of market entry and exit decisions, and the role of market interactions. It is obvious that in a general model of firm behavior, such aspects should complement a realistic analysis of the investment decision itself.

The theoretical literature on these issues has expanded dramatically during the last decade. For example, modern theory of investment under uncertainty (as reviewed by Dixit and Pindyck (1994)) stresses the fact that investment timing in general, and firm entry or exit in particular, are endogenous events. Theoretical models of firm behavior that allow for endogenous exit decisions have been developed for example by Jovanovic (1982), Hopenhayn (1992) and Ericson and Pakes (1995). These models also address the question of how market entries and exits of individual firms shape the evolution of an industry's structure over time. Given the advanced state of theory in this field, empirical models that take the endogeneity of exit decisions into account explicitly (rather than ignoring it or dealing with it in an *ad hoc* fashion) are still quite rare. I discuss models with endogenous entry and exit decisions in turn.

Empirical studies of plant or firm entry decisions

While most empirical models of industry dynamics focus on the evolution of an industry that is characterized by endogenous exit decisions (see below), there is also considerable interest in the determinants of market entry. Most models in the industrial organization (IO) literature focus on strategic aspects in game-theoretic set-ups[12], but there are also a few intertemporal optimization models that focus on entry decisions and plant or firm creation. Empirical evidence on entry decisions, however, is very sparse. Examples of intertemporal optimization models of market entry are Dixit (1989), Hopenhayn (1992), Ericson and Pakes (1995), and Das and Das (1996). The study by Das and Das, for example, is interesting because it considers the dynamics of both entry and exit of firms in the presence of entry adjustment costs that are sunk once the firm enters a market.

The fact that there are only very few empirical studies of market entry decisions is not surprising because information on firms that have not yet entered a market is hard to come by. Only in very specific situations can firms' pre-entry decisions be observed, and important pre-entry state variables such as (expected) profits are also unobservable (in particular for firms that have *not* entered a market). Geroski (1991) provides both a

[12] In the IO literature, there is an extensive discussion on entry deterrence, i. e., on strategies that incumbent firms can follow to affect market conditions in their favor in order to prevent potential entrants from actually entering. This literature dates back to Bain (1956) and Sylos-Labini (1962); a review can be found in Geroski (1991).

theoretical discussion of these issues and many empirical results; Siegfried and Evans (1994) provide a survey of this literature.

Dunne *et al.* (1988) provide extensive descriptive evidence on plant creation in the U.S. manufacturing sector (based on comprehensive plant-level data from the Longitudinal Research Database). Using these plant-level data, they were the first to provide a detailed analysis of entry and exit patterns (while earlier studies had to rely on net entry rates at an industry level). They find that "there is significant variation in the entry patterns and in the subsequent size and exit patterns for different categories of entrants" (p. 513). Note that these results have been important also for the development of theoretical models of industry dynamics such as the Ericson and Pakes (1995) framework.

Successful econometric studies of firm or plant entry include Berry (1992). His central idea is to use observed entry decisions of airlines as indicators of underlying profitability. Another example for the empirical application of models of industry dynamics with endogenous entry is a simulation study by Siow and Zhu (1997). Their model is based on the industry dynamics framework by Ericson and Pakes (1995). However, they also consider training and managing at the plant level (in fact, managing needs are the driving force for plant creation in their model). Siow and Zhu derive value functions and exit rules in a standard fashion; plant creation occurs by branching of existing single-plant or multi-plant firms. From their model, they can calculate invariant distributions and characterize cross-section dynamics of plants and firms. They derive a specification for which their simulation is consistent with plant-level data from the U.S. chemical industry.

Dunne *et al.* (1997) present empirical evidence on firm and plant using plant-level data from the Longitudinal Research Database. They show that firm entry is an important mechanism for introducing new technologies. Their findings correspond to theoretical findings on the introduction of new technologies by, *inter alia*, Lambson (1991) and Caballero and Hammour (1994).

The role of exit decisions in empirical investment models

When models of firm investment are estimated using panel data, the researcher usually faces some sort of panel attrition, resulting in unbalanced panels. There are several reasons for panel attrition: A firm or plant might leave a market or go bankrupt, it may be sold to a new owner, or firm representatives might just refuse to fill in questionnaires any more. Only the last event can reasonably be considered as random (although in some instances there might be some sort of endogeneity involved). All other forms of panel attrition must be considered as endogenous (non-random) events. The empirical relevance of exits (particularly, exits at the plant level) has been emphasized by Dunne *et al.* (1988, 1989). Hence, any researcher has to address the resulting selection problems in one way or another.

The first approach is to derive assumptions under which panel attrition can be dealt with using standard panel methods. Blundell *et al.* (1996) argue that when firm lifetimes are exponentially distributed and the selection process has a stable correlation with the investment model, then attrition bias is basically a firm-specific effect and can be differenced out in the econometric procedure applied to the panel. A sufficient condition for exponential distribution of firm lifetimes is that there is no duration dependence and that there are no time-varying regressors in the conditional probability of exit. Although these assumptions may be warranted in many applications (especially when panels are rather short), they are likely to be violated when exit decisions are driven by financial constraints, because these are likely to depend on macroeconomic variables which vary over the business cycle.

A second approach used by applied researchers is to ignore the selection problem when estimating the model and to assess the direction of the resulting biases when interpreting the results. For example, Chirinko and Schaller (1995) – in a panel study of Canadian firms – note that "by eliminating firms for which data are not available for the entire sample period, we may introduce a survivor bias. Since survivors will tend to underrepresent young firms who are more likely to face information problems in capital markets, our procedure tends to be biased against finding evidence of financial constraints" (p. 529). Such an argument suggests that many studies tend to reject the null hypothesis of no financial constraints *despite* the biases introduced by ignoring panel exits. Still, it would be interesting to see just how important this effect is, especially when policy recommendations are to be derived.

Any analysis which goes beyond these *ad hoc* approaches requires an explicit theory of market entry and exit decisions and a structural estimation strategy (see Abowd *et al.* (1995) for a detailed discussion). When empirical work is based on an explicit theory of entry and exit, unbalanced panels (reflecting observed market entries or exits) provide the opportunity to gain a more complete understanding of firm dynamics. Hence, entry and exit should not necessarily be considered as a problem for the panel econometrician.

There are only few empirical studies that are firmly based on explicit theoretical models of market dynamics. However, a general framework for the empirical analysis of firms' joint investment and exit decisions has been suggested by Pakes (1994). This model will be described in Section 3.3.1. It is based on the model of Markov-perfect industry dynamics constructed by Pakes and Ericson (1990) and Ericson and Pakes (1995). This framework focuses on the impact of uncertainty that arises from investment in research and development, and derives investment and exit rules for incumbent firms. Then it adds an entry rule and finally aggregates the optimal behavior of all firms, including potential entrants, into a rational expectations, Markov-perfect industry equilibrium. Econometric methods available for models with market interactions are discussed in Section 3.2.2.

Note that there is only one empirical application of such methods so far, the study of productivity dynamics in the U.S. telecommunications equipment industry by Olley and Pakes (1996). Their empirical model of firm behavior explicitly takes into account the evolution of the whole industry (using the concept of Markov perfect industry equilibrium with continuation and investment as control variables). Hence, each firm's optimal behavior has to be derived given the behavior of its industry rivals. Olley and Pakes were also extremely careful to control for unobserved firm heterogeneity and endogeneity of input demands. For estimation, Olley and Pakes concentrate on a single industry, the U.S. telecommunication equipment industry. This industry was chosen because it was subject to both rapid technological change and major deregulation policies. The resulting restructuring process involved a fair amount of entries and exits and large changes in the sizes of incumbents. These features make the telecommunication industry a natural choice for estimating a structural model of industry dynamics. Olley and Pakes note that the unbalanced panel they constructed based on these industry selection criteria "contains almost three times the number of observations in the balanced panel" (p. 1280). This fact shows that the biases introduced by restricting empirical analyses to balanced panels will indeed be severe (at least for innovative industries). Note that the dynamic programming model used in this study (see Section 3.3) is similar in spirit – common to these models is the emphasis on (relative) productivity shocks as the driving force of firm (or plant) growth and exit.

Another careful study of exit dynamics is Das (1992). She develops a dynamic programming model of capital retirement which stresses fixed costs and the firm's expectations about market demand (i. e., the expected output price). The empirical study of optimal bus motor replacement by Rust (1987) is also explicitly based on an optimal stopping rule, and it forms the background for much of the literature on structural exit models as well as for the theoretical model and its empirical application presented in this study.

There is also an older (and larger) empirical literature on the determinants of firms' market exits which uses reduced-form approaches (see Siegfried and Evans (1994) for a comprehensive overview). Among others, Dunne *et al.* (1988, 1989) provide empirical evidence on the importance of entry and exit decisions for the analysis of firm (and industry) dynamics. McGuckin and Nguyen (1995) are concerned with both determinants and effects of plant ownership change. For the empirical investigation, a non-balanced panel of almost 30,000 LRD plants is used. They find that in general, ownership change is associated with plants which run at above-average productivity. When performing poorly, on the other hand, large plants are more likely to be purchased, rather than closed. Finally, transferred plants experience improvements in productivity performance. The findings of McGuckin and Nguyen indicate that plant closure is indeed not the only, and arguably not the most important, form a firm's market exit decision may take. Market exit might also mean just selling the plant. The reasons which lead to transferring a plant to a new owner, however, are different from those for closing it. Very roughly speaking, plants with above-average productivity tend to be sold, while plants which perform poorly are closed. The latter effect is rather weak and decreases in importance with plant size.

Another interesting aspect is the role of financial constraints for market exit decisions (or bankruptcy). This leads to Section 2.2 where such aspects are discussed.

2.1.4 Using plant-level data in empirical investment studies

In recent years, the use of plant-level, or establishment, data in empirical research both on firms' investment decisions and on more general aspects of firm behavior (such as models with explicit market interaction) has increased dramatically. This is a result of the increased supply of plant-level databases as well as increased demand by researchers working on empirical projects in many fields, such as macroeconomics, industrial organization, labor economics, and financial economics.

There are a number of reasons why plant-level data ought to be preferred to alternative data sources (such as balance-sheet data from databases such as Compustat), at least for the empirical analysis of pure investment decisions. There are, however, some disadvantages as well. I will discuss a number of these issues here, concentrating on points relevant for the empirical part of this study. McGuckin (1995) provides a broader discussion of the usefulness of establishment level data in applied economic research.

Aggregation biases in empirical studies of firm behavior

In most studies of firm behavior, aggregation biases are a problem (see McGuckin (1995) for an overview of this issue). In investment theory, it is standard to assume that a firm decides on the level of overall investment spending (possibly subject to financial or other constraints). Implicitly, it is assumed that the firm has one or more projects available and that it is, at the margin, indifferent between spending on any of these projects, hence they are treated as just a single investment. In reality, however, investment and exit decisions are usually made for individual projects (i. e., products or product ranges), and they are – at least partially – based on the productivity of each individual project. Hence, the desirable level of aggregation for empirical studies of investment decisions is the individual investment project. However, only in rare cases are such detailed datasets available to the researcher, and if they are, the availability of variables might restrict the scope of empirical studies to very specific (though often economically very interesting) questions.[13]

[13] Examples include the study of production and capital usage decisions in the cement industry by Das (1992) and the analysis of operating regimes in nuclear power plants by Rust and Rothwell (1995) and Rothwell and Rust (1995, 1997).

The next level of aggregation is the plant (or establishment) level. The question whether using even plant-level data introduces aggregation biases has a clear theoretical answer (yes), but it should be viewed mainly as an empirical issue. In many cases, the production of a single plant will be very focused, so that plant investment decisions can still be viewed as a reasonable approximation of individual investment projects; however, when plants are not very specialized such an approximation might be unsatisfactory.[14] By the same reasoning, it is an empirical question whether aggregation biases from using firm-level data are of relevance. There is a growing literature on this issue, and the overwhelming conclusion is that the dynamics of (among others) investment, labor demand, and job creation and destruction are much richer at the plant level than at the firm level.[15]

Given that the plant level is the lowest level of aggregation at which datasets for broad samples of the manufacturing sector are available, the safest choice is to use such plant-level data whenever possible. Hence, the plant level was chosen as the primary level of aggregation for the empirical applications of the dynamic programming framework presented in this study.

There are a number of related data requirements relevant for empirical studies of joint investment and exit decisions; they are also more likely to be met by plant-level data. In particular, market exits for some product or product range may go unobserved when firm-level data are used (where only aggregated figures can be observed for variables such as labor and material input, investment expenditure, value added, or gross revenue).

---

[14] The U.S. Census of Manufactures contains a measure, the "primary product specialization ratio", defined as the fraction of a plant's output that can be assigned to the plant's primary 7-digit product class (which in turn determines the plant's 4-digit industry classification). As 7-digit product codes are fairly detailed and production technologies for a given product at a given plant should not vary too much, this measure should reflect how focused production and technology at individual plants in a given industry are. This measure is reported for each plant-year observation. For the plant-level dataset used in this study, the distribution of primary product specialization ratios is reported in Table 4.8; the numbers indicate that in the vast majority of plants considered here, production is concentrated on very few products and hence relatively homogenous, while the product range within a firm (i. e., across different plants that are owned by the same firm) is typically much broader.

[15] See Davis *et al.* (1996) for an overview of this literature and many empirical results.

Moreover, when market exit decisions are central to an empirical study, firm or plant exits must be well documented. For example, market exit can take two distinct forms, either plant closure or plant sell-off. These should be distinguished in the data.[16] Finally, plant-level datasets such as the Longitudinal Research Database (LRD) used in this paper usually do not contain financial variables. Hence, if an empirical study investigates the effects of firms' financial situation on investment, it is necessary to link plant-level and firm-level data. How this can be done in practice will be discussed in Section 4.3.

Disadvantages of plant-level data

The main disadvantage of plant-level datasets is, arguably, that there are not enough of them available to researchers. While detailed plant-level information is available at most national statistical agencies, these datasets are for reasons of confidentiality either not available to the public at all or access is restricted. McGuckin (1995) discusses existing plant-level datasets and the access and confidentiality issues involved. He also notes that statistical agencies seem to be willing to increase access to plant-level databases, although this process is slow. A leading example is the Center for Economic Studies (CES) maintained by the U.S. Bureau of the Census where researchers have access to confidential microdata under institutional arrangements that prevent disclosure of individual data (a detailed discussion of the Longitudinal Research Database provided by the CES is the subject of Section 4.A.1).

Plant-level datasets offer much, but not everything a researcher might wish. This is a result of the fact that the underlying plant-level data – at least the more comprehensive databases compiled by national statistical agencies such as the U.S. Bureau of the Census's Longitudinal Research Database (LRD) – have been obtained for purposes other than to be used by researchers. There are two major drawbacks which result: First, sampling procedures are tailored primarily for the purpose of statistical reporting and not so much for empirical research, and second, important

[16] This is the case for the LRD, but not for many other datasets where in both cases firms would just be dropped from the panel. Results by McGuckin and Nguyen (1995) show that plant ownership change is quite frequently observed in U.S. manufacturing.

groups of variables are not available, most notably, financial variables or variables on firms' R&D activities.

Sampling problems are generally difficult to solve for a given database. Sometimes the weighting schemes used by statistical agencies for their own reporting are available, but in many cases their effects on empirical work are hard to assess. A particular problem is that small firms or establishments are sampled with lower probability in order to reduce the cost associated with surveys for the firm or establishment. (How this issue is handled by the U.S. Bureau of the Census and how it is reflected in the Longitudinal Research Database is discussed in Section 4.A.1.)

The second problem frequently encountered in plant-level datasets is that some variable of interest is not covered. For example, if the empirical model requires information on the financial status of a firm, the desire to use high-quality plant-level production and investment data leads to a serious problem if the plant-level dataset does not contain such financial information. Hence, there is a fundamental trade-off between the generally higher quality of plant-level production, cost, and investment data and the need for other variables that can be obtained at the firm level only.

One solution to the problem of missing variables is to link plant-level production, cost, or investment data with firm-level data from other sources. The approach taken in this study is to use data as disaggregated as possible for each type of variable. In particular, production and investment variables (the "real" sphere of the model of firm decisions) are available at the plant level, while information on the financial status of a firm is available only at the firm level. Finally, price deflators and capital depreciation rates can be obtained at the 4-digit and 2-digit industry levels, respectively.

One example for this approach is the study by Lichtenberg and Siegel (1991). For their estimates of productivity growth, they calculate firms' real output and input variables at the 4-digit SIC industry level using LRD data. Doing this, they avoid diversification biases present in other studies of productivity growth. In a second step, they aggregate these real variables to the firm level and use firm-level data from another source to investigate the impact of alternative forms of R&D finance on productivity growth.

It should be noted, however, that matching and merging of datasets recorded at different levels of aggregation require considerable time and effort and may still result in relatively small sample sizes and in selection problems. These problems are difficult to assess when designing a research project (as detailed information on confidential plant-level datasets cannot be obtained in advance). For these reasons, there are still only very few empirical studies which follow this approach, and most of these studies restrict their attention to a small sub-sample of the universe of all establishments covered by plant-level datasets. The empirical application of the dynamic programming model of investment and market exit presented in Chapter 4 is no exception in this respect; it should be viewed as an illustration of what can (and cannot) be achieved given a limited amount of research time. The process of linking plant and firm-level data is discussed in detail in Section 4.A.2.

2.2 Firm investment under financial constraints

In this section, I discuss different aspects of firms' investment decisions under financial constraints. According to Modigliani and Miller (1958), a firm's financial decisions have no effect on its real investment decisions if there exist complete capital markets with perfect information. Once these latter requirements are not fulfilled, however, a firm's financial status may well affect its investment decisions[17], and this link, in turn, might have important effects at an aggregate level, as part of the transmission mechanism that explains real effects of monetary disturbances.

I begin with established theoretical models of informational asymmetries between borrowers (firms) and lenders (banks) that lead to credit rationing, or more generally, to financial constraints on firms' decisions. Then I review the literature on the macroeconomic consequences of such constraints, and the empirical evidence available so far. Finally, I present a more recent literature on the within-firm allocation of funds; these models have important implications for empirical studies of firm behav-

[17] The financial structure of firms influences other aspects of firm behavior as well. For an overview of the literature on interactions between financial structure and product market behavior, see Maksimovic (1996).

ior under financial constraints that use disaggregated data (such as the one presented in Chapter 4).

2.2.1 Informational asymmetries, credit rationing, and financial constraints

There are several reasons why rationing may occur on credit markets. Firstly, credit rationing can occur due to credit controls imposed by the authorities, for example as a means of monetary policy. The second form of credit rationing is disequilibrium or short-run rationing, which occurs when lenders adjust the interest rate they charge only slowly after external conditions have changed. Finally, credit rationing might occur because financial markets differ from goods markets in several ways. In particular, there exist informational asymmetries between borrowers and lenders. From an economist's point of view, the case of credit rationing resulting from informational asymmetries is the most interesting one as it occurs in equilibrium.

A model of adverse selection

Stiglitz and Weiss (1981) investigate informational asymmetries on financial markets by modelling the riskiness of the borrowers' projects as the main unobserved factor. Banks granting loans are concerned about the interest rate they receive on the loan, and the riskiness of the loan. But the interest rate a bank charges may itself affect the riskiness of the pool of its loans. Stiglitz and Weiss give two main explanations for this result:

- Adverse selection effects arise because a higher loan rate affects the borrowers with lower risk (who anticipate they will always repay the loan) more than it affects the riskier borrowers (who will recognize that the loan rate does not matter in situations where they have to default the loan). In an extreme case, a firm which is quite sure that it will not repay the loan because its project is very risky might accept any interest rate offered by the bank.[18] Adverse selection

[18] Jaffee and Stiglitz (1990), p. 858, point out that this result is even more relevant in a competitive setting in which loan applicants apply to several banks: "If one bank then raises its quoted loan rate, it knows that only those borrowers who have been refused loans at all other banks will accept its loans."

leads therefore to sorting of potential borrowers: At higher interest rates, only firms with risky investments will decide to borrow.

- Incentive or moral hazard effects may arise, i. e., the interest rate charged by banks might influence the actions of borrowers. When the interest rate increases, borrowers are willing to undertake riskier projects.[19]

The analysis by Stiglitz and Weiss (1981) concentrates on the adverse selection effects of informational asymmetries.[20] They show that given such effects, there exists a maximum rate of interest at which banks are willing to offer credits. Hence, raising the interest rate at any given level does not lead to a proportionate increase in the expected return to the bank. If the rate is raised beyond some endogenous threshold, expected returns decrease, as only borrowers with high risk projects are willing to accept such rates. Clearly, no bank will be willing to charge more than this rate. But the notion of a maximum interest rate charged by banks readily explains why credit rationing occurs in this model: Whenever the market-clearing interest rate (where overall supply and demand would be equal) is higher than the threshold, demand for credits exceeds supply. Then, some firms are rationed. Note that the model by Stiglitz and Weiss concentrates on adverse selection on credit markets. Similar results on the role of adverse selection have been obtained by Myers and Majluf (1984) for equity markets.

The model of Stiglitz and Weiss has been criticized because it fails to explain the use of debt contracts and because of the simple structure of loan contracts assumed. While Stiglitz and Weiss concentrate on rationing, there are other forms of agency costs that affect investment. In Gale and Hellwig (1985), for example, underinvestment occurs because of expected bankruptcy costs when firms differ in quality. One way to overcome informational asymmetries is to establish institutions that provide publicly available information on companies or, at least, provide this information at lower cost due to scale economies in information gathering (see Diamond (1984)). However, Williamson (1986) and others show that even

---

[19] This effect can be exacerbated by strategic considerations of firms operating in imperfectly competitive product markets, see Fudenberg and Tirole (1986).

[20] For an overview of models in which moral hazard problems lead to credit constraints, see Bester and Hellwig (1987).

with monitoring, credit rationing occurs in equilibrium (mainly because of monitoring costs). See Hellwig (1990) for an overview of the literature on monitoring and financial constraints, and Hubbard (1998) for a discussion of the literature on informational imperfections and investment.

Taking monitoring into account, the effects of informational asymmetries may not be severe as one regards large companies. For several reasons, however, matters are different for small firms. Firstly, gathering the necessary information on small and medium size businesses and individuals might well be difficult or too expensive relative to the small amounts of the loans. Secondly, increased firm size leads to reduced default risk because of diversification. Finally, the terms of contracts with small borrowers are likely to be very simple and, moreover, identical for different borrowers (think of standardized contracts). Consequently, financial constraints should be most severe for small firms persuing only few projects, for newly established firms, or for firms which aim to introduce new products. One should therefore expect credit rationing to be most severe for innovative firms engaging in R&D (see, e. g., Himmelberg and Petersen (1994)). How small firms are affected by financial constraints has been analyzed, for example, by Mankiw (1986), using the example of college students who apply for loans, with unobservable quality and no tangible collateral at hand. I return to this study below.

The models of credit market imperfections mentioned so far are essentially static in nature. In the more general multi-period case, explicit solutions are difficult to obtain, and there are few studies of optimal loan contracts in such settings (examples are Gertler (1992) and Lucas and McDonald (1992)). So far, both macroeconomic applications and empirical studies of credit market imperfections and firms' real economic activities are (implicitly) based on static models.[21] Typically, such studies derive the existence of financial constraints from static models and continue by imposing an exogenous restriction on the availability of external finance in the dynamic model of firm behavior. From a theoretical point of view, this practice is not entirely satisfactory, but the analytical problems involved resist explicit solutions (see Milne and Robertson (1996), p. 1428, for a discussion).

[21] I take up macroeconomic implications and empirical studies of credit market imperfections below.

Positive welfare effects of credit rationing

As Blanchard and Fischer (1989) note, "the term rationing automatically creates the impression of nonoptimality" (p. 485). Indeed, much of the discussion so far stressed the negative effects of credit rationing or, more generally, financial constraints. I conclude this section with more favorable views of financial constraints before taking up macroeconomic aspects in the next section.

There are several extensions to the original model of Stiglitz and Weiss. Most studies confirm that informational asymmetries distort the credit market equilibrium – hence, credit rationing should be considered socially harmful. However, changing the underlying assumptions can lead to quite different effects of credit rationing. De Meza and Webb (1987), for example, show that there will be *too much* investment in the credit-rationed equilibrium. Whereas in the original Stiglitz-Weiss model asymmetric information gives rise to an adverse selection problem that causes projects which are poor from the bank's point of view to drive out good projects, in the model of de Meza and Webb good projects draw in bad. Thus, there is too much investment and a subsidy on interest income could restore social efficiency.

There are also some studies which show that credit rationing can be socially efficient when there are informational asymmetries. These studies point out that credit rationing might be an efficient method of preventing investment in risky projects that would otherwise be undertaken because outside providers of funds have incomplete information. In particular, recent years have seen a surge of models that analyze the role of informational asymmetries not only between a firm and outside providers of finance (this aspect is at the heart of the credit rationing literature following Stiglitz and Weiss (1981)), but also within the firm, i. e., between managers and owners. I do not have the space here to review this literature in any depth; Shleifer and Vishny (1997) provide a survey of the literature on corporate governance.

However, given such informational asymmetries, Jensen (1986, 1993) has stressed that lenders can play an active role in disciplining managers by restricting the supply of outside funds. The central idea is that managers tend to act in their self-interest which might mean that they follow projects that yield utility for managers, but whose returns are too low for the owners, relative to alternative investments. In this sense, financial constraints need not be uniformly harmful, but can also help to alleviate within-firm incentive problems, eventually reducing the efficiency losses associated with overinvestment in risky projects. Also, by stopping to provide funds, the financial system can help to reduce excess capacity in declining industries, a task Jensen (1993) claims internal control systems are unable to fulfill. The extent to which these effects lead to an increase in aggregate welfare is still subject to debate, however (see, e. g., Shleifer and Summers (1988) for a different view on this issue).

2.2.2 Financial constraints and aggregate economic activity

In the recent macroeconomic literature, credit rationing and financial constraints received much interest.[22] This section reviews the literature on three related issues. First, a number of models argue that imperfections in capital markets, resulting, for example, in credit constraints, can explain the transmission of monetary shocks through the economy. This literature advocates a *credit channel* of monetary policy transmission (as opposed to the earlier view of a *money*, or *interest rate*, channel). Second, and more generally, imperfections on financial markets can exacerbate business cycle fluctuations by propagating all kinds of macro shocks; this literature suggests the *financial accelerator* as a new explanation of the longstanding "small shocks, large cycles" puzzle of macroeconomics. Finally, there is a literature which argues that beyond business cycle fluctuations, problems of asymmetric information such as credit rationing can lead to the collapse of the entire financial sector of an economy. The effects of capital-market imperfections on investment play a central role in much of this literature; Hubbard (1998) provides an overview. I discuss these issues briefly to show that the empirical evidence on the link between a firm's financial status and its investment decisions presented in Chapter 4 is important for this macroeconomic literature, too.[23]

---

[22] However, the notion of a link between capital market imperfections and real economic activity dates back to, at least, Irving Fisher's (1933) debt-deflation theory.

[23] The discussion here and in the empirical study presented in Chapter 4 focuses on equipment investment. There is also a growing literature on financial constraints,

The credit channel for monetary policy

Of central interest in macroeconomic theory is the monetary transmission mechanism, i. e., the economic mechanism by which movements in monetary aggregates can affect real economic activity.[24] Much of the traditional research has concentrated on the pure *money* channel of monetary transmission, while recent research has stressed the existence of a second channel, the *credit*, or *lending*, channel. There is some disagreement on whether these channels should be viewed as independent of each other. While Kashyap and Stein (1994) stress that these are indeed distinct channels for monetary transmission, Bernanke and Gertler (1995) argue that the credit channel should not be viewed as independent of the traditional monetary transmission mechanism, but rather as "an enhancement mechanism". (At the same time, they concede that it might already be too late to change the money vs. credit channel terminology.)

The traditional channel of monetary transmission works, in its most simple Keynesian textbook version, as follows. A contraction in money supply leads to a rise in real interest rates, which in turn raises the cost of capital, causing a decline in investment spending, and finally a decline in aggregate demand and a fall in output. The credit channel, on the other hand, is based on the view that monetary policy affects real activity via bank lending. There are several versions of the credit channel model which mainly differ in how a monetary contraction affects bank lending. The standard version argues that a monetary contraction reduces bank lending via reducing bank deposits. There is also a "monetarist" view in which movements in asset prices are pivotal in this process (see Taylor (1995)). Most studies, however, concentrate on the effects of incomplete information on bank lending: A monetary contraction either distorts equity prices (as in the monetarist view) or reduces firms' cash flows; in any case, this exacerbates adverse selection and moral hazard problems and hence reduces bank lending. Finally, there is a version of the credit channel model that focuses on consumer, rather than firm, spending on durable assets.

---

inventory investment, and aggregate activity, see, *inter alia*, Carpenter *et al.* (1994) and Kashyap *et al.* (1994).

[24] I do not attempt to review empirical evidence on the non-neutrality of monetary aggregates here; see Kashyap and Stein (1994) and Oliner and Rudebusch (1996) for recent overviews.

Following Mishkin (1995), Table 2.1 contains stylized versions of these money and credit channel models (and also of the "exchange rate channel" advocated, *inter alia*, by Obstfeld and Rogoff (1995)). In addition to Mishkin, see Kashyap and Stein (1994) and Hubbard (1994) for detailed discussions of the money vs. credit views of monetary transmission. Other recent contributions to this literature include Greenwald and Stiglitz (1993), Gertler and Gilchrist (1994), Meltzer (1995), Taylor (1995), and Bernanke *et al.* (1996). The latter paper takes a slightly more general view by identifying a "financial accelerator" which has implications for the propagation of macro shocks beyond the transmission of monetary policy.

For the purpose of this study, the central idea of most credit channel models is to extend microeconomic models of informational asymmetries between borrowers (for specificy, firms) and banks, by considering how the resulting financial constraints vary over the business cycle, and how they contribute to the propagation of nominal shocks through the economy. This idea had been around for some time; for example, Stiglitz and Weiss (1987), extending their 1981 model, find "that monetary policy may have a much larger effect on investment if the economy is in a credit rationing regime than if it is not" (p. 30). Jaffee and Stiglitz (1990) point out that "variations in the availability of credit can have large effects on real economic activity, both on the aggregate level and on its distribution among sectors and even individual projects. In addition, most would argue that monetary policy should be carried out, or at least measured and evaluated, with regard to its effect on the availability of credit" (p. 884). The main contribution of the more recent literature on the credit channel, therefore, is a formal link of microeconomic asymmetric information problems and macroeconomic issues such as the transmission of monetary shocks.

A central testable implication of credit channel models is that the availability of external funds (i. e., bank loans) influences firms' investment decisions. Note that this implication relates only to a single step of these models, the effect of bank lending on firm investment (see the stylized versions of these models in Table 2.1). For testing this implication, it is irrelevant how exactly a monetary innovation affects bank lending, be it via asset prices, cash flows, or asymmetric information problems (or, indeed, some combination of these). While this provides a powerful test

Table 2.1: Some stylized models of the monetary transmission mechanism

The *interest rate* or *money channel*:		Money supply ↓
	⇒	Real interest rates ↑
	⇒	Investment spending ↓
	⇒	Output ↓
The *exchange rate channel*:		Money supply ↓
	⇒	Real interest rates ↑
	⇒	Value of the domestic currency ↑
	⇒	Net exports ↓
	⇒	Output ↓
The *credit channel*,		Money supply ↓
bank deposit version:	⇒	Bank deposits ↓
	⇒	Bank lending ↓
	⇒	Investment spending ↓
	⇒	Output ↓
The *credit channel*,		Money supply ↓
asymmetric information version I:	⇒	Equity prices ↓
	⇒	Adverse selection, moral hazard ↑
	⇒	Bank lending ↓
	⇒	Investment spending ↓
	⇒	Output ↓
The *credit channel*,		Money supply ↓
asymmetric information version II:	⇒	Real interest rates ↑
	⇒	Cash flow ↓
	⇒	Adverse selection, moral hazard ↑
	⇒	Bank lending ↓
	⇒	Investment spending ↓
	⇒	Output ↓
The *credit channel*,		Money supply ↓
household expenditures version:	⇒	Equity prices ↓
	⇒	Likelihood of financial distress ↓
	⇒	Consumer durables, housing spending ↓
	⇒	Output ↓

Source: Adapted from Mishkin (1995), pp. 4–9.

for any credit channel model that focuses on firm investment, it is more difficult to assess the relative importance of alternative versions of the credit channel view. How this implication has been tested in empirical studies is the subject of Section 2.2.3, and some new evidence is presented in Chapter 4.

Credit constraints and financial collapse

Mankiw (1986) studies the macroeconomic implications of credit constraints faced by small firms or individuals, and he addresses the question whether government intervention could enhance efficiency in credit markets. He uses the example of college students who apply for loans. This is the prototype of a small, growing business: Quality is not (perfectly) observable, and there is no tangible collateral. Mankiw emphasizes two central results (p. 455). Firstly, "the equilibrium resulting in an unfettered market is inefficient and can be improved by government intervention ... even if the government has no informational advantage over lenders." Secondly, "the unfettered market equilibrium is precarious: small changes in the exogenous risk-free interest rate can cause large and inefficient changes in the allocation of credit."

Various government interventions are conceivable in order to restore efficiency. One possibility is the introduction of a credit subsidy which would effectively reduce the interest rate faced by borrowers. In Mankiw's model, such an intervention would have two effects. Firstly, some of the students with high returns and high repayment probabilities who were previously not investing would now do so; this effect is socially beneficial. Secondly, some other students with low returns and low repayment probabilities are induced to invest – which is socially harmful. In the first place, this result might not seem very encouraging for the government. But in order to evaluate the net social impact of a credit subsidy, the government only needs to know the distribution of individual repayment probabilities in the population; it is not necessary to distinguish high-return from low-return students. It might well be possible, as Mankiw shows in an example, that the extra investment generated is on net socially optimal but is not undertaken in the market equilibrium.

Finally, Mankiw shows how an increase of the market interest rate could lead to a financial collapse as the equilibrium in which lending is profitable for banks disappears. The investment projects might still be socially profitable at the higher interest rate, but none of the investors is able to raise the necessary capital. The same result may arise from an increase in the riskiness of some potential borrowers. This is one of the important results of Mankiw's paper: Even small changes in risk perception can have large effects upon the allocation of credit. Hence, a potential for financial collapse can arise not only from increases in the interest rate, but also from changes in the perceived riskiness of investment projects.

This potential for financial collapse has important macroeconomic implications. In the textbook IS-LM model, a monetary contraction precludes marginally productive investment. In this alternative model of credit allocation which emphasizes the credit rationing on individuals and small businesses, restrictive monetary policy could have more drastic effects. The higher interest rate can cause the collapse of the credit market, even though the projects of some borrowers remain socially productive at the higher interest rate. As Mankiw points out, his model emphasizes the propensity of financial markets for instability and collapse. He concludes: "At times, it is necessary for the government to remove some risk from the private sector by guaranteeing certain financial arrangements" (p. 469).

2.2.3 Empirical evidence on investment under financial constraints

In this section, I review empirical tests of the influence of financial constraints on firms' investment decisions. In particular, I try to identify areas where further research seems warranted.

Standard tests for financial constraints at the firm-level

The early empirical literature on financially constrained firms focused on the leading special case, credit rationing (defined as a situation in which borrowers cannot borrow as much as they would like given an unconstrained optimization model with complete financial markets). It is clear that finding empirical evidence on whether credit rationing exists is difficult even in absence of any measurement problems: Only the amount of credit that is actually transacted can be observed, but – by assumption – not the amount that is demanded.

A standard approach to deal with this problem is to estimate a reduced-form equation of firm investment which includes some variable assumed to reflect credit rationing, or more generally, the firm's financial situation. This approach has been introduced by Fazzari *et al.* (1988). They use cash-flow as a proxy for the availability of internal funds. The hypothesis to be tested is that the investment of firms which are rationed on credit markets is more sensitive to variations of internal funds than the investment of firms that are not subject to credit constraints. As discussed in Section 2.1, the typical reduced-form investment equation explains investment as a function of Tobin's q (i. e., the ratio of firm value and capital stock) which is the central determinant of firm investment in standard neoclassical models, and cash flow. They construct several versions of this model, but the investment equation basically explains investment as a function of average $\tilde{q}$ (as a proxy for the unobservable marginal q) and cash flow, Π.

$$\frac{i_t}{k_t} = \alpha_0 + \alpha_1 \tilde{q}_t + \alpha_2 \frac{\Pi_t}{k_t} \tag{2.12}$$

Note that investment and cash flow are normalized by the capital stock to account for size effects. For estimation, Fazzari *et al.* use firm-level panel data and split the sample into three subsamples according to the dividend payout ratio. This allows them to test whether the investment of low-payout (i. e., financially constrained) firms is sensitive to the availability of internal funds (by testing the hypothesis that α_2 is positive). Such a finding would then be interpreted as indicating that firms which are constrained on markets for outside finance are restricted in their investment decisions: Investment decisions depend not only on an investment's marginal value to the firm, but also on the availability of *internal* funds. Generally speaking, Fazzari *et al.* conclude that financing constraints affect investment. Their results are most dramatic for those firms in their sample described as new or relatively small. Assuming that credit rationing is even more severe for really small businesses which were not included in the sample, their results suggest that asymmetric information problems affect small firms to a high extent.

Following Fazzari *et al.* , there has been a host of empirical studies of the sensitivity of firms' (real) behavior to the availability of outside finance. These studies extend the original Fazzari *et al.* framework along various dimensions, using different firm-level datasets, different classification schemes for a firm's financial situation, different econometric techniques and different measures of firms' economic activity (i. e., decisions other than investment, such as inventory and labor input decisions). As a general result, most firm-level studies find that firms' behavior is sensitive to the financial situation. Bernanke *et al.* (1996) present a comprehensive overview of this literature.

Recent contributions include Hubbard *et al.* (1995) and Gilchrist and Himmelberg (1995, 1998). The paper by Hubbard *et al.* uses an Euler-equation based GMM estimation strategy (see below) and tests alternative specifications that could potentially rationalize the apparent failure of standard Euler-equation investment models. (In addition to financial constraints, these are tax payments and the free cash-flow hypothesis). Their results are consistent with the earlier findings by Fazzari *et al.* (1988). The papers by Gilchrist and Himmelberg use a very elaborate vector autoregression framework to construct an alternative proxy for the expected discounted stream of marginal profits, thereby overcoming some deficiencies of the traditional q-theory framework. Based on their sophisticated approach, Gilchrist and Himmelberg (1995) conclude that investment responds to cash flow even though the empirical approach controls for the role of cash flow as a forecasting variable for future investment opportunities. Gilchrist and Himmelberg (1998) extend this analysis by constructing two new forward-looking variables that enter their investment equation: a measure of the firm's fundamental q and a "financial q" that reflects the fact that the firm's discount rate depends on the shaddow value of being financially constrained in future periods.

Calomiris *et al.* (1994) interpret leverage as a state variable for firms' decisions. The choice variables they consider include, in addition to investment, also employment and inventories. They find that "firms that use debt to expand operations aggressively during booms are likely to be among the least creditworthy if a recession strikes, and may be forced to contract activity more than their rivals" (p. 2).

However, not all authors share the view that financial constraints and credit rationing are of much empirical relevance in the aggregate. Berger and Udell (1992), for example, analyze individual loan contracts and conclude that "the data suggest that equilibrium rationing is not a significant macroeconomic phenomenon" (p. 1947). Eichenbaum (1994) criticizes the study by Kashyap and Stein (1994) and a number of other empirical studies that support the credit channel view; his objections are mostly methodological. His main concern is that studies using macro data require strong identifying assumptions. First, one needs to isolate a measure of exogenous movements in monetary policy, and second, one needs an assumption that the supply of, rather than the demand for, credit has moved in response to a monetary shock. He concludes that the evidence is "equally consistent with alternative interpretations that stress the economic determinants of the observed heterogeneity among economic agents, like small and large firms" (p. 256).

An important policy issue that has been addressed in this literature is whether young, small, and/or R&D intensive firms are particularly likely to face financial constraints. There is not much empirical evidence on the effects of credit constraints for small firms. An exception is a paper by Gertler and Gilchrist (1994) who investigate the macroeconomic effects of credit constraints and provide empirical evidence on the different responses of small and large firms to monetary policy shocks (however, their main interest is in inventory rather than capital investment). They conclude that "small firms account for a significantly disproportionate share of the manufacturing decline that follows thightening of monetary policy" (p. 309). Finally, Himmelberg and Petersen (1994) confirm that R&D investment of small firms is influenced considerably by financial constraints.

Structural models of firm investment and financial constraints

As discussed in Section 2.1, an alternative to reduced-form estimation is to derive testable relationships from structural models of firm behavior. The resulting intertemporal optimality conditions (Euler equations) link marginal adjustment costs in adjacent periods and do not depend on the unobserved shadow value of capital. From these Euler equations, moment restrictions can be derived, and estimation is performed by the generalized method of moments (GMM). Whited (1992) and Bond and Meghir (1994) show how such structural models can be used to test for financial constraints. The basic idea is that the restrictions implied by standard neoclassical investment models should hold for *a priori* unconstrained firms across adjacent periods, whereas for constrained firms there should exist a wedge between the marginal cost of investment today vs. investment tomorrow. Another example for this approach is the paper by Hubbard *et al.* (1995) already mentioned.

One of the main conceptual advantages of approaches based on an Euler equation is that they do not rely on Tobin's q and hence are not affected by its mismeasurement. While structural models of the type discussed here are widely believed to be superior to reduced-form models for theoretical reasons, their empirical performance is mixed.

Financial constraints, investment, and endogenous market exit

Other issues that recently received some attention are the role of financial constraints in models with endogenous exit decisions, and aggregation biases in the empirical analysis of investment decisions. These are common themes of the empirical approach taken in this study, and I refer to the discussions in Sections 2.1.3 and 2.1.4 for theoretical arguments why these issues are important.

There is some recent empirical evidence on the role of financial constraints for market exit. Kovenock and Phillips (1995, 1997) analyze the effects of financial restructuring on firms' investment and market exit decisions using a reduced-form approach. They focus on the interaction of firms' capital structure decisions and plant closure/investment decisions. Such an analysis is related to Jensen's (1993) claim that capital market pressure helps firms to reduce excess capacity caused by demand shocks and changes in productivity. They build their study on the maintained hypothesis that capital structure is a choice variable of the firm.

Kovenock and Phillips have to address one of the problems of the LRD database discussed in Section 2.1.4 – the absence of any financial information. Using external sources (such as Compustat, the Wall Street Journal Index and lists of firms that were subject to leveraged buy-outs compiled by other authors), they identify firms that underwent major capital structure changes. Based on this information, Kovenock and Phillips select ten industries in which at least one out of the top four firms was affected by major capital restructuring.

Based on this sample, Kovenock and Phillips perform logit regressions on a binary variable that indicates whether a plant was shut down in a particular year. The independent variables capture firm and market conditions (such as capital structure changes, plant level efficiency, demand conditions, and market structure). They also do regressions of investment variables on the same set of independent variables. In particular, they use a Logit regression with the dependent variable indicating whether capital expenditures increased by more than 5% in a given year, and a Tobit regression of investment levels (which are left-truncated at zero). Kovenock and Phillips find that capital structure (i.e., high leverage) has significant effects on investment and plant closure when the industry is highly concentrated. Moreover, after capital restructurings, plant closures are more likely and firms invest less. Summing up, Kovenock and Phillips present strong evidence for the relevance of a firm's financial situation for its investment and market exit decisions.

Finally, Holtz-Eakin *et al.* (1994) analyze entrepreneurial survival in the presence of financial constraints using a rather descriptive approach. Their results are consistent with the notion that liquidity constraints exert a noticeable influence on the viability of small, innovative (in their terminology, "entrepreneurial") firms.

On balance, the literature discussed in this section suggests that accounting for endogenous exits should be a fruitful addition to the literature on investment under financial constraints.

The identification of constrained firms in empirical studies

To conclude this section, I mention very briefly a common conceptual problem encountered in empirical tests of investment under financial constraints: How can financially constrained firms be identified? Most of the standard empirical tests for real effects of financial constraints emphasize cross-sectional differences in effects of internal funds on firms' investment. There is, unfortunately, no straightforward way to identify financially constrained firms, because the intended investment decisions (i. e., the investment decisions that would have been taken without financial constraints) are not observable. Most existing studies use simple criteria to split their samples into sub-samples of firms considered as subject to financial constraints or as unconstrained. Examples are the dividend payout ratio or firm size. However, such indirect approaches have some serious drawbacks; Hubbard (1998) provides a detailed discussion of the issues involved. A recent example for an effort to construct a direct measure of financial constraints is Calomiris and Himmelberg (1998); they use data firms' underwriting costs which are a major component of the cost of external financing.

The issue of identifying financially constrained firms is one of the central concerns of the empirical study in Chapter 4, and a detailed discussion is therefore deferred to Section 4.2. There, I also introduce an alternative measure for firms' financial status that has recently been proposed by Kaplan and Zingales (1997).

2.2.4 The within-firm allocation of funds for investment

The advantage of the diversified corporation is often thought to reside in its ability to locate capital internally more efficiently than can be done with external capital markets. For example, Williamson (1975) argues, "assignment of cash flows to high yield uses is the most fundamental attribute of the M-form enterprise" (p. 148). However, the recent literature on the theory of the firm stresses the importance of within-firm incentive problems for the decisions of larger companies with several divisions (see Montgomery (1994) for an overview of the issues). This literature has important implications for empirical studies of firm investment under financial constraints: It suggests that not only the overall level of a firm's investment spending is influenced by financial constraints, but also the allocation of financial funds among different projects, plants, or divisions of the firm.

Harris and Raviv (1996) stress the fact that a firm's investment decisions are affected by incomplete information not only via constraints on the availability of external funds, but also via within-firm incentive problems in the allocation of funds to different projects: "To understand the investment behavior of firms, one must consider both the process by which external capital is made available to firms and the process by which internally and externally raised capital is allocated to investment projects within the firm." (p. 1139) They argue that both problems are ultimately due to incomplete information: External capital market frictions result from asymmetric information between the firm and potential lenders, and internal incentive problems result from decentralized information about the expected returns of alternative investment projects.

As discussed in the previous sections, the effects of the availability of outside funds on firm investment have received much attention both theoretically and empirically. The problem of the within-firm allocation of funds, however, has been largely ignored for some time, and only recently has a research program emerged that takes up this issue. This literature concentrates on internal capital markets, and more generally, the firm's capital budgeting process under incomplete information. In a string of recent papers (e. g., Gertner *et al.* (1994), Stein (1997), Shin and Stulz (1996)), financial economists have investigated optimal mechanisms for the allocation of funds, with special emphasis to internal capital markets.

Stein (1997), for example, stresses the fact that corporate headquarters, by virtue of their control rights over sub-divisions, can engage in "winner picking", i. e., they can actively shift funds from one project to another. One implication of their model is that even when the firm's relationship with the outside capital market is subject to agency problems that result in firm-wide credit constraints, these can be relaxed by optimally allocating funds within the firm.

Another interesting aspect is the role of diversification or divestiture in the presence of imperfect capital markets. Such models have important implications for the empirical analysis of plant closure or sell-off decisions. Ofek (1993), for example, stresses that "high leverage increases the probability of discontinuing unprofitable operations, laying off employees, and replacing inefficient management" (p. 6). Matsusaka and Nanda (1996) develop a model of the multidivisional firm and investigate the firm's decision whether to remain diversified or split into single-business firms (refocus). They find that "refocusing can be an optimal response to increased efficiency of external capital markets and increased competition in the firm's home market".

Empirical evidence on the within-firm allocation of funds

There is also some empirical evidence on the allocation of funds across investment projects, or, at an intermediate level of aggregation, among different subsidiaries of a large corporation. The volume by Ravenscroft and Scherer (1987), for example, provides extensive empirical evidence on mergers and sell-offs in the United States (in particular, during the merger waves of the 1960s and early 1980s), with special emphasis on the question whether mergers and sell-offs promote economic efficiency.

One interesting implication of the theories presented above is that if a large firm is hit by a negative cash-flow or outside finance shock, the effects on investment spending are spread out across all projects (or subsidiaries). As data on the allocation of funds within firms are difficult to obtain[25], most empirical studies are extensive case or event studies. The strategy used in these empirical tests is based on the identification

[25] As discussed in Chapter 2.1.4, there are comprehensive datasets on firms' plant-level production and factor input (including investment) decisions; but in most cases, financial aspects are not covered by these data.

of some external shock to the cash position of a firm that does not affect its investment opportunities (i. e., Tobin's marginal q).[26] In the case of Blanchard *et al.* (1994), these shocks are "cash windfalls" resulting from won or settled lawsuits, while Lamont (1997) investigates the effects of the 1986 oil price decrease that reduced the cash position of oil companies.

The study by Blanchard *et al.* concentrates on firms without attractive investment opportunities and the related literature on free cash-flow (Jensen (1986)). They argue that their data support agency models of firm behavior in which managers' objectives differ from those of shareholders. Their sample consists of 11 firms which are known to lack attractive internal investment opportunities (judged by their low q's and low investment in own businesses even after the windfall). Hence, the windfall corresponds to free cash-flow in the sense of Jensen. The main finding is that these firms indeed keep the additional cash within the firm, wasting it on low-return projects, or paying out cash only to managers and large blockholders.

Lamont's (1997) main finding is that the finance costs of different parts of the same corporation are interdependent. In particular, if one division of a large corporation is hit by a shock to its cash flow, such as in the case of the oil price shock that affects oil companies, the effects are spread out over the entire company, even to non-oil subsidiaries. Shin and Stulz (1996), on the other hand, find that relative allocations of funds in diversified firms are sticky. Using Compustat data and a relatively large panel of firms, they fail to find support for the view that diversified firms allocate more funds to divisions in industries with better investment opportunities. Also, they find that investment in small divisions of firms is related to the cash flow of other segments.

Implications for empirical studies of firms' investment decisions

The literature on internal capital markets has important consequences for the analysis of firm investment under financial constraints: In the case of large corporations, the researcher needs to investigate not only whether outside financial constraints affect firms' overall level of invest-

---

[26] These studies can therefore be considered as good examples for "natural experiments" in the sense of Meyer (1995).

ment activity (as measured by balance-sheet capital stock and investment variables), but also how funds are allocated between alternative projects *within* the firm. It is clear that data on this latter issue are much harder to obtain. The empirical study presented in Chapter 4 can address part of the within-firm allocation problem by using plant-level investment data that are combined with firm-level financial data, but unfortunately, the databases used do not contain any direct information about the within-firm flow of funds; Section 4.3 contains details.

2.3 Non-standard constraints and firm behavior: a research program

I conlcude this chapter with an outline of a research program for the empirical analysis of firms' investment decisions. The analysis of the literature in Section 2.1 revealed that the empirical performance of the standard neoclassical investment model is not quite satisfactory; this is true for both reduced-form approaches based on, say, Tobin's q, and for structural approaches which exploit Euler equations.

The standard intertemporal optimization model of investment has been extended along various dimensions. Judging from the evidence available so far, some of these extensions help to explain empirical stylized facts of investment decisions, such as the sluggish response to exogenous shocks (which cannot be fully explained by convex adjustment costs). These extensions are:

- an explicit role for uncertainty and an option value of waiting;
- non-convex adjustment costs;
- irreversibilities;
- lumpiness of investment projects;
- market interactions and endogenous exit decisions.

In Chapter 3, I will argue that each of these extensions to the standard intertemporal optimization model of investment can be treated in a consistent framework, based on Markov decision processes. Moreover, while investment is, *prima facie*, a continuous choice variable for the firm, the underlying structure of discrete projects suggests that investment decisions are to a large part discrete in nature.[27] Therefore, the empirical analysis in this study uses a dynamic mixed discrete-continuous model of investment and exit, resulting in a discrete dynamic decision process. I would argue that the empirical analysis of the above-mentioned extensions to the standard investment model should also be conducted using such a framework.

The second important area of investment research is concerned with the role of financial constraints. Here, I would also argue that in order to assess the effects of a firm's financial situation on investment spending, one needs to look at the level of individual projects, or at least at disaggregated within-firm data. Doing this requires a thorough understanding of investment decisions, and again the extensions to the standard investment model described above seem to be important.

The analysis of the literature in Section 2.2 has shown that there are some attempts in this direction, but what seems to be missing is a consistent framework in which the effects of financial constraints on investment decisions can be analyzed. The dynamic programming model of investment decisions seems to be an interesting approach, although many practical problems remain to be solved.

The theoretical model of joint investment and market exit decisions developed in Chapter 3 and the empirical application in Chapter 4 should be seen as steps in that direction.

[27] This was also one of the main motivations for Rust's (1987) work on dynamic discrete-choice models.

Chapter 3

A dynamic programming framework for the analysis of firm decisions

In this chapter, I present a dynamic programming model designed for the empirical analysis of firm behavior under various non-standard constraints. The main purpose of the model is not to serve as a tool for the theoretical analysis of firms' investment decisions, but to give empirical studies a solid foundation in recent theoretical advances in this field. Hence, the model is quite stylized in some respects (such as its focus on discrete decision variables). Its general structure, though, allows it to be readily adopted in empirical studies of firm behavior, using advanced structural estimation procedures that are firmly based on the underlying optimization model. The analysis starts from the observation that a firm's market entry and market exit are endogenous events in a general model of firm behavior. In the model presented here, I do not analyze the determinants of entry and exit in an explicit market-interaction framework, but emphasize the endogeneity of the firm's market exit decision in a model of investment behavior. In such a framework, market interactions are reflected implicitly in the firm's exit rule; they enter via the effects of equilibrium output prices on the firm's relevant state variables.

Section 3.1 contains an introduction to the theory of Markov decision processes (MDPs). I will also discuss methods for the numerical solution of both continuous and discrete MDPs, and I show how the framework can be extended to allow for occasionally binding inequality constraints (such as irreversible investment or financial constraints). In Section 3.2, I review methods for the econometric estimation of Markov decision processes. I concentrate on methods for models with discrete choices, and in particular, on Rust's (1987, 1988) nested fixed-point algorithm (NFXP). In Section 3.3, these tools are put to work in an empirical model of firm investment which incorporates endogenous exit decisions. Some mathematical results are collected in Appendix 3.A for quick reference.

3.1 An introduction to Markov decision processes

This section contains a brief introduction to the theory of dynamic programming (DP) in general and to Markov decision processes (MDPs) in particular. The latter can take the form of continuous decision processes (CDPs), discrete decision processes (DDPs), or mixed discrete-continuous decision processes (although in this study the latter are approximated by specifying a corresponding discrete decision process). The aim of this section is to establish some notation and a few results for general MDP problems that will be useful in subsequent sections where a DDP model of investment and market exit decisions and techniques for econometric estimation of DDPs are derived. The presentation will be non-technical, and the reader will frequently be referred to the appendix or to the original literature for further details and technicalities. The discussion generally focuses on the infinite-horizon case as the investment model used in this study assumes an infinite planning horizon. References for the finite-horizon case will be given in passing.

Before turning to substantive matters, here are some notes on the literature. The classical reference on dynamic programming is Bellman (1957). The standard textbook on DP techniques has been Bertsekas (1976) for almost two decades; more recent texts are Puterman (1994) and Bertsekas (1995). DP methods have been widely used in economics in recent years. Stokey and Lucas (1989) is an introduction to the use of recursive methods in various areas of economics. Rust (1994d) and Rust (1996) provide more specialized introductions to MDP methods in economics; the focus of the former is on econometric estimation, while the latter covers computational aspects of MDP simulation and estimation. Macroeconomic applications of MDP methods can be found in two volumes by Sargent (1987, 1996).

3.1.1 Sequential decisions and Markov decision processes

This section contains a general formulation of Markov decision processes and discusses their relationship to intertemporal (sequential) decisions of economic agents.[28] I begin by characterizing the agent's intertemporal decision problem in general terms. The framework allows for quite different economic applications, firms' joint investment and market exit decisions analyzed in this study being only one example. Other applications include individual or household decisions on portfolio choice, saving, retirement, or migration. Specific applications can be formulated using both discrete and continuous state and control variables, a finite or infinite planning horizon, and assuming perfect or imperfect state information. In the following, I will restrict attention to Markovian problems (to be defined shortly) and to discrete time, although non-Markovian set-ups such as continuous-time semi-Markov models are conceivable as well; see An (1995).

Table 3.1: The primitives of a Markov decision process

- A discrete time index, $t \in \{0, 1, 2, \ldots, T\}, T \leq \infty$.
- State variables and a state space, $s_t \in S$.
- Control (decision) variables and a decision space, $a_t \in A$.
- A family of constraint sets, $A_t(s_t) \subseteq A$.
- A family of (Markov) transition probabilities[a],
  $p_t(\mathrm{d}s_{t+1}|s_t, a_t) = \mathrm{Prob}(s_{t+1} \in \mathrm{d}s_{t+1}|s_t, a_t)$.
- A family of single period utility functions, $u_t(s_t, a_t)$.
- A discount factor $\beta_t(s_t, a_t) \in [0, 1)$.
- A utility functional with additively separable decomposition,
  $U(s, a) = u_0(s_0, a_0) + \sum_{t=1}^{T} \left[\prod_{\tau=1}^{t-1} \beta_\tau(s_\tau, a_\tau)\right] u_\tau(s_\tau, a_\tau)$.

Source: Rust (1996), p. 632.

[a] Formally, the transition probability $p(\mathrm{d}s'|s, a)$ maps $\mathcal{B}(s)$, the Borel σ-algebra of measurable sets of S, into the unit interval.

The intertemporal optimization problem

The Markov decision process framework builds on the observation that under suitable assumptions, an economic agent's intertemporal decisions can be characterized, in mathematical terms, as a Markov decision process. The primitives of her decision problem are summarized in Table 3.1. The agent is assumed to be characterized by a vector of state variables, s_t, and by a vector of decisions (actions), a_t, at each point in

[28] The material presented in this section is mostly based on Rust (1996).

time ($t = 1, \ldots, T; T \leq \infty$). Her current utility is given by a utility function $u_t(s_t, a_t)$ that has both the current state and the actions she takes as its arguments. Further, this period's actions affect the distribution of next period's state variables via a Markov transition probability $p_t(ds_{t+1}|s_t, a_t)$.

Definition: Stationary Markov decision processes

A Markov decision process given by the objects listed in Table 3.1 is stationary if:

1. The transition probabilities and utility functions are constant over time:
   $p_t(s_{t+1}|s_t, a_t) \equiv p(s'|s, a)\,, \quad \forall t\,,$
   $u_t(s_t, a_t) \equiv u(s, a)\,, \quad \forall t\,.$

2. The discount factor is independent of states and actions and constant over time:
   $\beta_t(s_t, a_t) \equiv \beta\,, \quad \forall t\,.$

In the remainder of this section, I assume that the Markov decision processes considered are stationary.[29]

The intertemporal optimization framework assumes that the agent seeks to maximize her expected life-time utility subject to a family of state-dependent constraint sets, $A_t(s_t) \subseteq A$, and that her life-time utility has an additively separable representation. Hence the agent solves, in period $t = 0$, the following problem:

$$\max_{\alpha} E_{\alpha} \left\{ \sum_{t=0}^{T} \beta^t u(s_t, \alpha_t) | s_0 \right\} . \tag{3.1}$$

Here, E_α denotes that expectations are taken with respect to the controlled stochastic process $\{s_t, a_t\}$ induced by the optimal policy $\alpha =$

[29] To simplify notation, I drop time subscripts and use primes to denote next period's values where no confusion arises (as is standard in the dynamic programming literature).

$\{\alpha_0, \ldots, \alpha_T\}$, given the initial state s_0. More explicitly, the optimization problem can be stated as follows:

$$\max_{\alpha} \int_{s_0} \cdots \int_{s_T} \sum_{t=0}^{T} \beta^t u(s_t, \alpha_t)$$
$$p_0(\mathrm{d}s_0) \prod_{t=1}^{T} p(\mathrm{d}s_t | s_{t-1}, \alpha_{t-1}) , \tag{3.2}$$

where p_0 is the probability distribution over the initial state, s_0. The solution to this problem is a sequence of policy functions, $\alpha = \{\alpha_0, \ldots, \alpha_T\}$. These policy functions are state-dependent, i. e., they generally depend on the whole history of past state variables. Below, I discuss how this problem can be solved in the finite-horizon case ($T < \infty$) and in the infinite-horizon case ($T = \infty$).

The general framework used so far allows for both discrete and continuous Markov decision processes. In the case of a discrete decision process (DDP), the decision space is a finite set A such that $A(s) \subset A$, for all $s \in S$. For a continuous decision process (CDP), $A(s)$ is a compact subset of $I\!R^{|A|}$ with non-empty interior (for all $s \in S$). In general, the solutions (i. e., policy functions) of MDP models are elements of (a subset of) an infinite-dimensional Banach space $B(S)$.[30] Mixed discrete-continuous decision processes, i. e., decision processes with both discrete and continuous control variables, can be treated as special cases of DDPs for the purposes of this study; for this, the continuous control variable needs to be discretized. If this discretization is sufficiently fine, the continuous control can be approximated perfectly.[31] An alternative approach to solve mixed discrete-continuous problems is to use appropriately modified methods for CDPs such as Euler equation approaches. This method is discussed by Pakes (1994), and I return to this issue below (see Section 3.1.2).

---

[30] Formally, let $B(S)$ denote the Banach space of all measureable, bounded functions $f : S \to I\!R$ under the (essential) supremum norm, $||f|| = \sup_{s \in S} |f(s)|$. Again, I supress measurability issues in the following. See Rust (1996), p. 621, for details.

[31] In fact, any CDP could be solved by the discretization methods described for DDPs below. However, this approach is subject to the "curse of dimensionality", and other methods are preferred for the solution of problems with only continuous controls. See Rust (1997) for a discussion.

The finite-horizon case and backward induction

Consider first the finite-horizon case with an exogenously given planning horizon. In the last period, T, the optimal policy is given by

$$\alpha_T(s_T) = \underset{\alpha_T \in A(s_T)}{\arg\max} \left[u(s_T, a_T) \right]. \tag{3.3}$$

For periods $t = 0, \ldots, T-1$, optimal policies can be obtained simply by backward induction, namely

$$\alpha_t(s_t) = \underset{\alpha_t \in A(s_t)}{\arg\max} \left[u(s_t, a_t) + \beta \int V_{t+1}(s_{t+1}) p(\mathrm{d}s_{t+1} | s_t, a_t) \right] \tag{3.4}$$

$$V_t(s_t) = \max_{\alpha_t \in A(s_t)} \left[u(s_t, a_t) + \beta \int V_{t+1}(s_{t+1}) p(\mathrm{d}s_{t+1} | s_t, a_t) \right]. \tag{3.5}$$

Equation (3.5) is known as the finite-horizon *Bellman equation.* Backward induction implies that the value function in the planning period, $t = 0$, represents the maximized expected discounted value of utility in all future periods and that the decision rule $\alpha = (\alpha_0, \ldots, \alpha_T)$ is indeed optimal (see Rust (1996), p. 634).

The infinite-horizon case: stationarity and Blackwell's theorem

In the infinite-horizon case, the planning horizon is $T = \infty$, and there is no last period to start backward induction from. Recall that in general, the solution to (3.2) is an optimal decision rule $\alpha = (\alpha_0, \ldots, \alpha_T)$. Without further assumptions, the infinite-horizon decision rule lies in an infinite-dimensional space of sequences of potentially history-dependent functions, and each evaluation of the objective function requires $(T+1)$-fold multivariate integration (Rust (1996), p. 633). To make the model tractable, it is necessary to impose additional structure on this general version, and the most important simplifying assumption is that of stationarity.

The stationarity assumption leads to a significant simplification in the infinite-horizon case: The future looks the same whether the agent is in state s_t at time t or in state s_{t+j} at time $t + j$ provided that $s_t = s_{t+j}$. Hence, the agent's optimal decision rule and corresponding value function will be time-invariant (Rust (1996), p. 634). An important implication of the stationarity assumption is that the discount factor is constant. This seems quite natural in the context of an individual's intertemporal utility maximization where β corresponds to her rate of time preference and hence is a deep (structural) preference parameter; when applying the MDP framework to firms' decisions, matters get more complicated, as the discount factor reflects the interest rate which is generally time and even state-dependent. Where appropriate, I discuss how cases in which stationarity does not hold trivially can be dealt with; examples are models with occasionally binding inequality constraints on the choice set (Section 3.1.4) and models of firm behavior with time and state-dependent discount factors (Section 3.3.2).

The proof of existence and uniqueness of an optimal policy in a Markov decision process requires certain regularity conditions, the most important of which (for economic applications) are summarized in the following assumption:

Assumption MDP: Regularity conditions for Markov decision processes

For a Markov decision process given by the objects listed in Table 3.1, the following regularity conditions are assumed to hold:

1. The MDP is stationary.
2. The state space S and the decision space A are compact metric spaces, and A is convex.
3. $s \rightarrow A(s)$ is a continuous correspondence.
4. The utility function $u(s, a)$ is jointly continuous in (s, a) and quasiconcave in a.
5. The discount factor is $\beta \in [0, 1)$.

For economic applications, the most important regularity conditions concern stationarity, a (time-constant and state-independent) discount factor bounded away from unity, and the boundedness of the utility function $u(\cdot)$. Although there is a version of Blackwell's theorem (Bhattacharya and Majumdar (1989)) that does not require that the utility function be bounded, we maintain this assumption throughout this study because it is still required by the numerical solution methods presented below.

The solution of such a dynamic decision problem is a (sequence of) policy functions $\alpha_t : s_t \rightarrow a_t$, defined implicitly by (3.1) or (3.2). In the case of a stationary MDP, the policy functions will be stationary as well, hence the sequence of optimal policy functions is given by $\alpha = (\alpha(s), \alpha(s), \ldots)$. It can be obtained by solving the functional equation, $V = \Gamma(V)$, where the Bellman operator $\Gamma : B(S) \rightarrow B(S)$ is defined as:

$$\Gamma(V)(s) = \max_{\alpha \in A(s)} \left[u(s,a) + \beta \int V(s') p(\mathrm{d}s'|s,a) \right] . \tag{3.6}$$

Equation (3.6) is known as the Bellman equation; it is the infinite-horizon analogon to equation (3.5). Its solution is mathematically equivalent to the fixed point of the functional equation $V = \Gamma(V)$, and existence and uniqueness of such a fixed point can be established by a version of the contraction mapping theorem (stated in the appendix). The fact that Γ is indeed a contraction mapping is, in turn, ensured by two sufficient conditions established by Blackwell and hence known as *Blackwell's sufficient conditions*: monotonicity of Γ and a discount factor β that is bounded away from unity. Blackwell's famous (1965) theorem (see the Appendix) establishes that the stationary decision rule induced by the solution to the Bellman equation is an optimal decision rule for the underlying optimization problem (3.2) in the infinite-horizon case.

In all but the most simple applications, there does not exist an explicit analytical solution to the functional equation (3.6).[32] For a class of continuous Markov decision processes, the solution to the Bellman equation can be characterized conveniently in terms of a stochastic *Euler equation* (to be defined shortly); in all other cases, numerical solution methods are required. These methods are the subject of the next two sections.

3.1.2 Euler equations for continuous Markov decision processes

In this section, I discuss solution methods for continuous Markov decision processes (CDPs). I concentrate on a class of CDPs for which a first order condition that characterizes an optimal decision rule α and that does not depend on the value function V exists. This fact allows to bypass solving the Bellman equation numerically. Using the envelope theorem, one can transform this first order condition into a functional equation

[32] Rust (1996), pp. 636–9, gives examples of simple economic problems in which the Bellman equation has a closed-form solution.

for the optimal policy α; this functional equation is known as an Euler equation.

Note that in most cases, the Euler equation does not provide a closed-form solution for the decision rule α. It can be used, however, to derive moment conditions for econometric estimation (using the generalized method of moments (GMM), discussed below in Section 3.2). Finally, and very briefly, I discuss methods for the numerical solution of CDPs for which no closed-form solution exists. More details on stochastic Euler equations can be found in Stokey and Lucas (1989), Chapters 9 and 10; the material presented here is adapted from Rust (1994c).

Bellman and Euler equations for CDPs

To interpret the Euler class of continuous decision processes (CDPs) in the general framework of Markov decision processes used in this study, a number of technical assumptions are necessary; these are stated formally in Table 3.2.

The vector of state variables, $s = (y, z)$, consists of two components, an endogenous state variable, y, and an exogenous state variable, z (both might be vectors of state variables). The law of motion for the exogenous state variable is unaffected by the agent's action a. Assume that z follows a Markov process with a transition probability given by $q(\mathrm{d}z'|z)$. The endogenous state variable is affected by the agent's decision a via the law of motion $y' = g(y, a, z', z)$, a concave function. This function can be interpreted as a return function or as the intertemporal resource constraint that links state variables across adjacent periods.

In economic applications of continuous Markov decision problems, one might think of the state and control variables in terms of standard models of firm investment or household saving. The most simple case has just one control variable, one exogenous and one endogenous state variable; in economic applications, these might be:

- Control variable, a: investment or savings
- Exogenous state variable, z: revenue or income
- Endogenous state variable, y: capital stock or assets

Again, $g(\cdot)$ is the return function that determines the evolution of the endogenous state variable: In the case of firm investment, this is the standard capital stock recursion, while in the case of a household's savings decisions, it is the intertemporal budget constraint which reflects the household's interest income received on its assets held.

Table 3.2: The Euler class of continuous Markov decision processes

- The decision space A is a subset of $I\!R^M$.
- The state space is a product space $S = Y \times Z$, where Y is a closed subset of $I\!R^J$, and Z is a closed subset of $I\!R^K$.
- The constraint set $A(s) = A(y,z)$ is an upper hemicontinuous correspondence which is increasing in its first argument: $y \le y' \Rightarrow A(y,z) \in A(y',z)$.
- The constraint set $A(y,z)$ is convex in y: For all $z \in Z$ and all $y, y' \in Y$, if $a \in A(y,z)$ and $a' \in A(y',z)$, then for all $\mu \in [0,1]$: $\mu a + (1-\mu)a' \in A(\mu y + (1-\mu)y', z)$.
- The transition probability factors as: $p(\mathrm{d}s'|s,a) = p(\mathrm{d}y', \mathrm{d}z'|y,z,a) = I\left(\mathrm{d}y' = g(y,a,z',z)\right) q(\mathrm{d}z'|z)$, where $g(\cdot)$ is a concave function.
- For each (y,a,z',z), there exists an $M \times J$ matrix $h(y,a,z)$ that satisfies $\frac{\partial g(y,a,z',z)}{\partial y} = \frac{\partial g(y,a,z',z)}{\partial a} h(y,a,z)$.
- The utility function $u(s,a) = u(y,z,a)$ is a strictly concave function of y and a for all $z \in Z$.

Source: Rust (1994c), pp. 24–5.

Under the assumptions stated in Table 3.2, and using the fact that $y' = g(y, \alpha(y,z), z', z)$, the Bellman equation for this class of problems is

$$\begin{aligned} V(s) &= V(y,z) \qquad (3.7) \\ &= \max_{a \in A(y,z)} \left[u(y,z,a) + \beta \int V(g(y,a,z',z),z') q(\mathrm{d}z'|z) \right] . \end{aligned}$$

Note that concavity of u, A, and g implies that the Bellman operator maps (strictly) concave functions onto (strictly) concave functions. This, in turn, implies that the fixed point is strictly concave and can therefore be characterized by first-order conditions. Using the theorem on optimal decisions in Euler-class CDPs stated in the appendix, the following general form of the stochastic Euler equation can be obtained:

$$\begin{aligned} 0 &= \frac{\partial u(y,z,a)}{\partial a} + \beta \int \left[\frac{\partial u(y',z',a')}{\partial y} - \frac{\partial u(y',z',a')}{\partial a} h(y',z',a') \right] \\ &\quad \frac{\partial g(y',a,z',z)}{\partial a} q(\mathrm{d}z'|z) . \qquad (3.8) \end{aligned}$$

The Euler equation is a first-order necessary condition that characterizes the optimal decision rule, defined implicitly by $a = \alpha(y, z)$. The interpretation of the Euler equation is straightforward: The change in expected utility from a small change in the control variable (say, consumption) vanishes when the control is chosen optimally, $a = \alpha(y, z)$.

One can see that for Euler-class models, the optimal solution can be characterized in terms of current marginal utility and next period's expected discounted value of marginal utility – it is not necessary to consider the impact of current decisions on marginal utility (or profit) in all future periods, $t+2, \ldots$. Hence, the Euler equation (3.8) is a recursive formula that characterizes the optimal decision rule α, similar to the recursive characterization of V in (3.8). Just as the Bellman equation defines V as the fixed point to the Bellman operator $\Gamma(V)(s)$, the Euler equation defines the optimal decision rule as the fixed point to an Euler operator $\Phi(\alpha)(y, z)$. It is therefore not straightforward to find a closed-form solution for α; in general, it is not easier to solve the functional (Euler) equation (3.8) than to directly solve the functional (Bellman) equation (3.8). Moreover, the Euler operator is generally not a contraction mapping, and further conditions are required to prove uniqueness of the solution to an Euler equation in general (see Coleman (1991)). This fact limits the choice of numerical methods for solving the Euler equation.

Also, note that the above result requires that the optimal decision $\alpha(y, z)$ be an interior point of the constraint set $A(y, z)$. In the case where the maximizing value of a in (3.8) is on the boundary of the constraint set, the first order conditions are given by inequalities, and (3.8) is no longer valid. Instead, one would need to include state-dependent Lagrange multiplier functions $\lambda(y, z)$; solution methods for such models are discussed below in Section 3.1.4.

Numerical methods for solving continuous decision processes

Numerical solution methods are required for most economic applications of continuous Markov decision processes. This is the case when the implicit solution to a CDP given by the Euler equation is not sufficient for the research question at hand, when no Euler equation exists, or more generally, whenever no closed-form solution to the Bellman equation exists. In addition to some very simple models which have closed-form solutions, there is one important class of models with closed-form solutions: The class of linear-quadratic economies used by Sargent (1976) and a large subsequent literature (see Anderson *et al.* (1996) for a recent review).

There are two major approaches for the numerical solution of continuous Markov decision processes: Discrete and smooth approximation. Discrete approximation exploits the contraction property of the Bellman equation. The method uses successive approximation to search for the optimal value function over a finite grid that discretizes the (continuous) state and control space. Details on this approach and various refined versions of the algorithm can be found in Rust (1996). Note that the basic idea of discrete approximation is also used in the solution of discrete Markov decision processes, so some additional details are given below. There is, however, a major difference between the computional problems encountered in continuous and in discrete decision processes: Rust (1997) has shown that the underlying computational problem, Bellman's *curse of dimensionality*, cannot be solved in the case of continuous decision processes, while it can be solved for discrete decision processes by using a randomization procedure, see Section 3.1.3.

An alternative to discrete approximation is smooth approximation which is achieved by treating either the value function V or the optimal policy function α as smooth, flexible functions of the current state, s, and some finite-dimensional parameter vector. Such methods include orthogonal polynomials, interpolation, splines, neuronal networks, and other projection techniques. Judd (1996) discusses these methods in detail (in particular, see pp. 561–3 for applications to dynamic programming). Note that there is an ongoing debate whether smooth approximation methods should actually be preferred over discretization methods. Judd (1996) notes that discretization procedures are slow when compared to smooth approximation methods, while Rust (1996) stresses that discretization methods are essentially exact (provided the discretization is sufficiently fine) and might be prefered in many circumstances.[33]

[33] See Rust (1996), p. 624, for the discrete approximation position, and Judd (1994), p. 262, or Judd (1996), p. 514, for the smooth approximation view.

3.1.3 Numerical solution of discrete Markov decision processes

In this section, I discuss numerical methods for the solution of discrete Markov decision processes. These solution methods are ultimately intended to be used in the maximum likelihood estimation of dynamic decision processes (to be discussed in Section 3.2). Rust (1996), p. 622, notes that for such applications, speed, accuracy, and numerical stability are critical. The methods presented here are discrete approximation methods; they approximate the original DDP problem by a finite grid over the state space, S, while the decision space, A, is discrete by construction. Bertsekas (1976), pp. 180–91, provides regularity conditions for (piecewise linear) discrete approximation methods.

Note that in the finite-horizon case, the optimal solution can be obtained by backward induction (see Rust (1996), pp. 649–52). The integration in (3.2) reduces to simple summation over the cells of the discretized state space. In the following, I concentrate on the infinite-horizon case. The standard method for the infinite-horizon case is based on the idea of successive approximations (suggested by the contraction mapping theorem). I conclude with a discussion of some recently proposed randomization (Monte Carlo) methods that can be used to gain significant speed-ups in numerical solutions of DDPs. The main reference for this section is Rust (1996).

Successive approximation and Newton-Kantorovich iterations

Having established the existence and uniqueness of the Bellman function and the existence of the corresponding policy functions, a solution to the infinite-horizon discrete Markov decision process, the next step is to actually find this solution. As noted before, analytical solutions exist only in very limited special cases, so one has to resort to numerical methods. The solution to an infinite-horizon discrete MDP is a fixed point of Bellman's operator equation, $V = \Gamma(V)$, or equivalently, a zero to the nonlinear functional $F(V) = 0$, where $F = (I - \Gamma)$. The two main methods for computing fixed points to general contraction mappings are the *method of successive approximation* and the *Newton-Kantorovich method.* The method of successive approximations can be summarized by the following expression:

$$V_{i+1} = \Gamma(V_i) = \Gamma^{i+1}(V_0)\,, \tag{3.9}$$

where V_0 is an arbitrary starting value. The Contraction Mapping Theorem (see the Mathematical Appendix) implies that this method is globally convergent. An alternative method uses the Newton-Kantorovich iteration,

$$V_{i+1} = V_i - [I - \Gamma'(V_i)]^{-1}(I - \Gamma)(V_i), \tag{3.10}$$

where $\Gamma'(V)$ is the Fréchet derivative of Γ evaluated at the point $V \in B(S)$.[34] The main advantage of the Newton-Kantorovich method is that the iterations converge to V at quadratic rate, given a starting point V_0 in a domain of attraction of V, $||I - \Gamma(V_0)|| \leq (1-\beta)^2/(2K)$, where $||\Gamma''(V)|| \leq K$, for some constant K. This property suggests using a polyalgorithm like the one proposed by Rust (1988): Start with successive approximations and when an error bounds criterion indicates that the current iteration is sufficiently close to V, switch to the Newton-Kantorovich iterations to converge more rapidly to the solution V.

In the empirical study of Chapter 4, the method of accelerated successive approximations is used in a modified version of Rust's polyalgorithm (see Rust (1996), pp. 653–4, for details). This method uses the *McQueen-Porteus error bounds* to speed up the computation of the fixed point to the contraction mapping, $V = \Gamma(V)$. Suppose that V is the true solution, while V_0 is any initial starting estimate for the standard successive approximation method. Then after i successive approximations, it can be shown that the (unkown) true value of V must lie within upper and lower bounds given by:

$$\Gamma^i(V_0) + \underline{b}_i e \leq V \leq \Gamma^i(V_0)\bar{b}_i e, \tag{3.11}$$

where e denotes an $|S| \times 1$ vector of ones, and the error bounds are given by

$$\begin{aligned} \underline{b}_i &= \beta/(1-\beta)\min\left[\Gamma^i(V_0) - \Gamma^{i-1}(V_0)\right] \quad \text{and} \\ \bar{b}_i &= \beta/(1-\beta)\max\left[\Gamma^i(V_0) - \Gamma^{i-1}(V_0)\right]. \end{aligned}$$

The contraction property ensures that the error bounds approach each other geometrically at rate β. An improved estimate of V can therefore be obtained as soon as $|\bar{b}_i - \underline{b}_i|$ falls below some pre-specified tolerance,

[34] The Fréchet derivative is a bounded linear operator $\Gamma'(V) : B(S) \to B(S)$ with $||\Gamma'(V)|| \leq \beta < 1$.

and the new estimate is given by the median value of the bracket bounded by $\underline{b}_i$ and $\bar{b}_i$,

$$\hat{V}_i = \Gamma^i(V_0) + \left(\frac{\underline{b}_i + \bar{b}_i}{2}\right) e \,. \tag{3.12}$$

Alternative algorithms

There are a number of alternative deterministic algorithms that can be used to solve the fixed-point problem associated with the Bellman equation; Rust (1996) discusses, *inter alia*, accelerated successive approximations, policy iteration methods that focus on the optimal policy function α rather than on the value functional V, and state aggregation methods. Rust also compares the empirical performance of these algorithms for a test problem; generally, the choice of the "optimal" method depends on the specifics of the problem at hand, in particular on the dimension of the state space.

While the deterministic algorithms discussed so far are standard in the dynamic programming literature, recent research has focused on non-deterministic algorithms that involve simulation methods. Rust (1997) proposes a randomized version of the successive approximation algorithm and proves that this algorithm can break the curse of dimensionality for discrete decision processes. Geweke (1996), pp. 793–7, reviews Monte Carlo integration methods that can be used to compute the expectations entering value functions related to certain classes of Markov decision processes. Note, however, that these simulation methods have not yet been used in empirical applications.

3.1.4 Dynamic models with occasionally binding constraints

The next step of the analysis is to incorporate further restrictions into the dynamic programming model of economic behavior. In particular, I focus on inequality constraints which, in a dynamic setting, are not binding in every period. Economic applications include households' consumption and saving decisions under borrowing constraints (İmrohoroğlu (1989), Zeldes (1989), Deaton (1991), Hajivassiliou and Ioannides (1991, 1994, 1996), and Hartley (1996)), and firms' investment decisions. In the latter case, inequality restrictions can affect investment either directly, in the case of irreversibilities (see Christiano and Fisher (1997) and the discussion in Section 2.1), or indirectly, in the case of financial constraints (see Corres *et al.* (1997), Milne and Robertson (1996), and Section 2.2). Here, I discuss the consequences of such additional constraints for the numerical solution of Markov decision processes. First, I concentrate on continuous Markov decision problems as these are common in economic applications; later, I show how discretized versions of such models can be dealt with in the discrete Markov decision process framework. This approach has been advocated, *inter alia*, in a string of papers by Vassilis Hajivassiliou and John Rust, and I use it in the empirical model of firms' joint investment and exit decisions presented in Section 3.3.[35]

Continuous decision processes and irreversibility constraints

I begin with a discussion of solution algorithms for continuous decision processes with occasionally binding constraints; general discussions of numerical methods for models with such constraints can be found in Marcet (1994), Christiano and Fisher (1997) and McGrattan (1997). In the following, I use the case of irreversible investment to illustrate this approach, but the framework naturally extends to other inequality constraints such as financial constraints. Recall from Section 2.1 that irreversible investment has been analyzed extensively in the recent investment literature; most models use a continuous-time framework and a slightly different mathematical approach; here, I stick to the discrete-time set-up used throughout this study.

In a simple model of firm investment, there is an intertemporal resource constraint that governs the evolution of the capital stock over time,

$$k' = (1 - \delta)k + i\,, \tag{3.13}$$

where i is gross investment (the continuous control variable) and $\delta \in (0, 1)$ is the depreciation rate. In the general dynamic programming framework for continuous decision processes derived in Section 3.1.2, this is a special case of a state transition probability $p(x'|x, z, a)$, where the endogenous state variable is capital, $x \equiv k$, and the control variable is investment, $a \equiv i$. Note that there is also an exogenous state variable

[35] Examples are Hajivassiliou and Ioannides (1991, 1994, 1996) and Corres *et al.* (1997), using reduced-form estimation strategies; and Rust and Phelan (1997), using a structural approach. The econometric estimation of such models is the subject of Section 3.2.

z, and uncertainty is reflected by specifying some stochastic (Markov) process for z. For a complete description of the intertemporal investment model, further structural assumptions, e. g., on the form of the profit function, are required, but for the purpose of this section, they are not crucial. A complete model of firm investment along these lines can be found in Section 3.3.

How does irreversibility enter this framework? Suppose, for simplicity, that there are no markets for used capital at all. Then, investment is restricted to $i \geq 0$ instead of $i \geq -(1-\delta)k$. There is hence a restriction that gross investment cannot fall below zero, and this constraint will occasionally be binding – whenever the firm would like to reduce its capital stock by more than its physical depreciation in an unrestricted model.[36] This implies that the case of $i = 0$ can occur with positive probability.

Solution algorithms for models of this kind have been developed and compared by Christiano and Fisher (1997); see also Rust (1994c), pp. 123–29. As noted in Section 3.1.2, there are two basic approaches for solving a continuous decision process: Discrete approximation, where the optimal solutions are searched over a finite grid of the state and decision space (this is the classical dynamic programming approach), and smooth approximation methods.

In principle, it is possible to solve any dynamic optimization problem with occasionally binding constraints such as the irreversible investment model by discrete approximation (see Christiano and Fisher (1997), Appendix 1). The solution is obtained by value function iterations over a finite grid of the state space, and upon convergence of the value function, the optimal policy function is derived. The only difference to the standard successive approximation algorithm discussed in Section 3.1.1 is that the constraint set needs to be modified according to the inequality constraint. Examples for this approach are İmrohoroğlu (1989), she uses this method for a simple model of household consumption under bor-

[36] In the case of fully reversible investment, there is still the restriction that $i \geq -(1-\delta)k$, but when the profit function is bounded and the discount factor is bounded away from unity (both conditions are covered by the assumptions made for general dynamic decision problems in Section 3.1.1), one can show that it will never be optimal to drive the capital stock to zero so that the lower bound is not reached.

rowing constraints; and Hartley (1996), who applies a slightly modified value-function approximation method to a model of consumer demand for credit cards under borrowing constraints.

While this approach approximates the solution to the intertemporal optimization problem with inequality constraints as the finite grid becomes finer and finer, the numerical burden involved prevents solving more complicated models on standard computers. This is the reason why Christiano and Fisher compare, for this simple test problem, the exact dynamic programming solution with various smooth approximation solutions that greatly reduce the computational burden.

To illustrate the use of smooth approximation methods in this context, consider a minimal residual method based on the Euler equation for the investment model sketched above. For a given policy α, the Euler residual is defined as $R(\alpha)(k,z)$, given by the right-hand side of (3.8). Minimal residual methods search for the optimal policy $\alpha(k,z)$ by setting this residual to zero (over a suitable function space). The additional constraint can be handled by introducing a state-dependent Lagrange multiplier function $\lambda(k,z)$, and the Euler equation can be re-written as

$$R(\alpha)(k,z) - \lambda(k,z) = 0\,. \tag{3.14}$$

The solution to this new problem is given by two functions, $\alpha(k,z)$ and $\lambda(k,z)$, that satisfy (3.14) and the corresponding Kuhn-Tucker complementary slackness conditions. The optimization problem can, again, be solved by searching jointly for the two functions that set the new residual $R(\alpha)(k,z) - \lambda(k,z)$ to zero.

Christiano and Fisher (1997) discuss six alternative smooth approximation methods that work along these lines: three parameterized expectations approaches, a Galerkin-Chebyshev projection method, a Galerkin spline method, and a successive approximation method based on the Euler operator $\Phi(\alpha)(k,z)$ that corresponds to (3.14) (see Section 3.1.2 for the definition of that operator). The technical details of these approaches are not of interest here; the important point is that only the parameterized expectations approaches satisfy the Kuhn-Tucker conditions automatically, while accommodating the occasionally binding constraint is more difficult in the other frameworks.

It should also be noted that Christiano and Fisher make the optimization problem tractable by assuming a simple two-state stochastic process for the exogenous shock variable z, with a good state, z_g, and a bad state, z_b, and by imposing the assumption that the irreversibility constraint is binding only in the bad state. While this assumption has some appeal in theoretical models of irreversible investment where one could think of markets for used capital goods as breaking down only in a recession (the bad state), the continuous dynamic decision framework is difficult to use in empirical applications due to its restrictive assumptions. This is the reason why in the next section, I turn to discrete decision processes which are easier to handle in some empirical applications.

Discrete indicator variables for occasionally binding constraints

An alternative to the explicit solution of a continuous decision problem with occasionally binding constraints is to derive a mixed discrete-continuous model from the underlying optimization problem. In this model, an additional discrete (binary) indicator variable takes the value 1 whenever the constraint is binding. The central idea is to interpret the fact that the household or firm is constrained in a given period as an additional choice variable; this reflects that being constrained is an endogenous event in an intertemporal optimization problem. For the case of investment decisions under financial constraints, this approach is used by Corres *et al.* (1997), and for the case of consumption decisions under liquidity constraints, by Hajivassiliou and Ioannides (1994).

The latter paper also contains a formal characterization of the Markovian solution to a mixed discrete-continuous dynamic programming model with financial constraints. The existence of a unique solution to the corresponding value function can be proved using the general MDP apparatus discussed in Section 3.1.1, as all required assumptions hold in this set-up as well. In particular, Hajivassiliou and Ioannides (1994), pp. 12–3, show that the solution, an optimal policy for the continuous choice variable, is stationary (because the continuous choice is made conditional on the discrete financial constraints indicator). In this study, I use this framework for a mixed discrete-continuous model of a firm's joint investment and market exit decisions under financial constraints; see Section 3.3.

The stationarity property makes the mixed discrete-continuous model of economic behavior under occasionally binding constraints amenable to structural estimation using the econometric methods for discrete decision processes discussed in Section 3.2.3. Alternatively, Hajivassiliou and Ioannides (1994) and Corres *et al.* (1997) show how reduced-form approaches can be used to investigate the discrete choices implied by their consumption and investment models. Note that in both cases, it is necessary to observe whether a firm or household is constrained in the empirical data.[37] The econometric estimation of Markov decision processes in general, and the issue of reduced vs. structural estimation in particular, are the subject of the next section.

3.2 Strategies for the econometric analysis of dynamic decision processes

From the discussion in the previous section, it should be clear that models based on Markov decision processes allow deep insights into intertemporal decisions of economic agents (individuals as well as firms). There are, however, only relatively few empirical studies based on this framework to date. The main reasons are that econometric techniques for structural estimation of dynamic models are computationally burdensome and that they require both a host of auxiliary assumptions and very detailed and reliable data. This, in turn, makes empirical work time and cost intensive when compared with reduced-form approaches. Before turning to these issues and describing some structural econometric methods that are currently available, I begin this section with a brief comparison of reduced-form and structural methods for the empirical analysis of dynamic models.

3.2.1 Reduced-form vs. structural estimation

Reduced-form and structural approaches are related to the general framework of Markov decision processes described in Section 3.1 in the fol-

[37] Sometimes, this can be achieved by using external information that is matched with the main panel dataset that contains information on the remaining state and control variables. This is the approach taken in Chapter 4 for the case of firm investment under financial constraints. Japelli *et al.* (1997) contains an application to the analysis of consumption decisions: The main data are from the U.S. Panel Study of Income Dynamics, and the indicator variable for financial constraints is constructed from the Survey of Consumer Finances.

lowing sense. In MDP models, economic behavior can be described by a collection of realizations (over different individuals or firms, and over time) of the joint stochastic process of state and decision variables, $\{s_t, a_t\}$.[38] Reduced-form estimation can be characterized as summarizing the stochastic process that governs these observed variables by some statistical or econometric regression method. The objective of structural estimation is not so much to analyze the observed process $\{s_t, a_t\}$ itself, but to uncover the underlying preferences and beliefs of the decision-maker; in the notation of Section 3.1, these can be summarized by the tuple $(u(\cdot), p(\cdot), \beta)$ or, after choosing functional forms for $u(\cdot)$ and $p(\cdot)$, by a vector of "deep" parameters $(\theta_u, \theta_p, \beta)$.

Rust (1988) describes the structural approach as solving an inverse (or revealed preference) problem: Given an observed stochastic process $\{s_t, a_t\}$ that governs the states and decisions of a decision-maker, is there a set of beliefs and preferences (or, rather, parameters of the state transition probability and the utility function, $(\theta_u, \theta_p, \beta)$) for which $\{s_t, a_t\}$ coincides with the solution of an intertemporal optimization problem? And if so, can the researcher infer $(\theta_u, \theta_p, \beta)$ from observations of $\{s_t, a_t\}$?

Formally, the reduced form of an MDP is the agent's optimal decision rule, or, in this chapter's notation, $\alpha(\cdot)$. The structure of an MDP is the mapping $(\theta_u, \theta_p, \beta) \rightarrow \alpha$ that renders the optimal policy function for any specification of beliefs and preferences. This mapping is defined implicitly by the solution to the Bellman equation (3.6); see Rust (1994d), p. 3126.

The reduced-form approach for estimation of dynamic models

From the viewpoint of an applied researcher, an attractive alternative to the computationally often prohibitive structural estimation is to resort to reduced-form estimation methods. This approach concentrates on the

[38] For convenience, I supress notation indicating that realizations of variables are specific to individuals (as long as no confusion arises). In general, panel data summarize a stochastic process $\{s_t^i, a_t^i\}, i = 1, \ldots, I, t = t_0^i, \ldots, t_T^i$, observed for I individuals. Note that this formulation allows for unbalanced panels (reflected in different lengths of observed person or firm spells) and hence for endogenous entry and exit decisions such as retirement or market entry or exit. This in turn helps to avoid selection biases that would destroy the ability to estimate structural parameters for the population of interest. Also, note that a subset of $\{s, a\}$ may not be observable to the econometrician, although it is assumed to be known to the decision maker. I return to these issues below.

observable implications of a given dynamic model of individual behavior. To illustrate this approach, I concentrate on dynamic discrete-choice models.

The basic idea of reduced-form estimation is to derive optimal decision rules for one or more discrete (typically, binary) choices from the solution of the corresponding dynamic programming model (which might also include some continuous choice variables such as saving or investment). In the case of firm behavior, such discrete choices might be whether to start new investment projects (or, more simply, whether to choose net investment above some threshold level), whether to exit from a market, or whether to take some financing action, such as issuing bonds or new equity or paying dividends in a given year. Examples of discrete decisions of households that should appropriately be analyzed in a dynamic model are retirement decisions, the decision to quit a job in order to search for a new one, the decision whether to migrate within a country or to another country, the choice of durable consumption goods, or discrete aspects of savings decisions such as portfolio choice (and there are many more).

Given data on such discrete choices, the researcher can estimate the optimal choice policies as functions of a set of explanatory variables (suggested by the underlying optimization problem). The estimation of the choice probabilities can then proceed either individually, using, say, a standard Probit estimator, or (preferably) jointly, using some multinomial Probit estimator. At least in the latter case, estimating such models still requires some computational effort because the solution of the maximum likelihood problem involves computing multi-dimensional integrals for which no closed-form solutions exist. Usually, this problem is solved by applying some simulation method.[39]

An important advantage of the reduced-form approach is that generally, the empirical model can be specified richer than a corresponding structural model, allowing for more explanatory variables and less restrictive error structures. However, a researcher might feel tempted to add explanatory variables which do not have a clear role in the underlying intertemporal optimization problem; in that case, the intended close

[39] See Hajivassiliou (1993) and Stern (1997) for overviews of the literature on simulation estimation of dynamic multinomial probit models. Two important examples are the simulated maximum likelihood estimator by Börsch-Supan and Hajivassiliou (1993) and the simulated moments estimator by McFadden (1989).

relation between the underlying optimization problem and the empirical model can disappear quickly.

Reduced-form models can help the researcher to build some understanding for a given economic problem, especially, when he or she enters a new area of research where formulating and estimating structural dynamic models is difficult (see Pakes (1994), p. 244). The reduced-form study of the U.S. Social Security disability benefit application process by Benitez-Silva *et al.* (1998) is an example for this approach: The reduced-form results are used to check the validity of state variables that will enter the structural estimation of a much more complicated dynamic discrete-choice model of individual behavior in old age.

Generally speaking, reduced-from approaches are not likely to render efforts to estimate structural dynamic programming models superfluous: A carefully specified structural model has clear advantages when it comes to policy experiments because its implications are unaffected by the Lucas critique; this issue is discussed in the next section.

Policy evaluation and prediction using structural methods

I now turn to a brief discussion of how structural estimation methods can be used for policy evaluation, that is, for predicting the effects of a given policy change on individual behavior. In fact, the main justification for the use of complicated structural models instead of reduced-form approaches is the ability to derive valid predictions of individuals' reactions to proposed policy changes. In recent years, dynamic discrete-choice models have increasingly been used in policy analysis. This is due to the facts that many interesting economic decisions are of discrete nature, and that discrete choices (such as retirement or plant closure) are in many cases perfectly observable, while continuous choices (such as saving or investment) are typically subject to measurement error. Wolpin (1996) discusses examples of public policy analysis with dynamic discrete-choice models, and the April 1997 issue of the *Journal of Business and Economic Statistics* contains a collection of articles that use structural estimation methods in applied microeconomics (see Keane and Wolpin (1997)).

In the famous *Lucas critique* of deriving policy advice from reduced-form estimates of (macroeconomic) relationships, Lucas (1976) argues that reduced-form estimation uncovers only an economic agent's *historical* decision rule. The estimated decision rule can be used to predict the agent's behavior in the future, provided that the environment under which the historic behavior was observed does not change. However, if a policy change alters the agent's relevant environment, forecasts of her future behavior that are based on observed historic behavior are not valid. The effects of such policy changes, however, are exactly the ultimate objective of most empirical studies of economic behavior. Hence, there are serious doubts about the usefulness of reduced-form methods for policy simulations.[40] This point has been made, less explicitly but much earlier, by Marschak (1952) who stated that "if among the policies considered there are some that involve structural changes, then the choice of the policy best calculated to achieve given ends presupposes knowledge of the structure that has prevailed before", and he defines a structure as "a set of conditions which did not change while observations were made but which might change in the future" (p. 26, see also Wolpin (1996), p. 427).

The central idea of policy evaluation using structural estimation is to express the policies of interest in terms of a vector of parameters, ϕ, that shift agents' beliefs about future states, as summarized in the state transition matrix $p(\cdot)$; see Rust (1994d), p. 3086. Note that these policy parameters are different from the structural parameters that describe agents' preferences or technologies and their conditional expectations about future state variables. The latter parameters are called structural or deep parameters and are invariant to policy changes; hence, they can be estimated using data observed *under a given policy.* In terms of the MDP model developed in Section 3.1, the Markov transition probability can be written as $p(s'|s, a, \theta, \phi)$, where θ is the vector of structural parameters to be estimated. This estimation is performed using panel data $\{s_t, a_t\}$ observed under some given policy regime ϕ. The virtue of a well-defined and successfully estimated structural model of individual or firm behavior is that the deep parameters remain unchanged even after a policy change. Hence, using the values of $\hat{\theta}$ estimated under some policy

---

[40] Formally, Lucas showed that key equations in Keynesian macroeconomic models (such as the consumption, investment, and portfolio balance schedules), are not structural equations in the dynamic optimization model he suggested; in particular, the parameters of these equations are not invariant with respect to the class of policy interventions studied. – A formal discussion of the Lucas critique in a dynamic programming framework can be found in Sargent (1987a), pp. 40–41.

ϕ, the dynamic programming model can be re-solved for an alternative policy $\tilde{\phi}$ to predict behavior under the new policy.

Although for theoretical reasons, there is a strong case for using structural methods for the evaluation of the effects of policy changes, applications to real-world problems are still rare. There are two main reasons for this. First, there are serious practical problems associated with the structural approach. These are mainly due to the combination of computational complexity and the need for very detailed and reliable data. These difficulties can prevent using structural methods for a given research question, but they can be overcome in principle. Second, while reduced-form models are subject to the Lucas critique, the structural approach has some methodological problems of its own: Its validity depends on the assumptions that agents are rational expected-utility maximizers and that the corresponding structural model of intertemporal decisions (such as the Markov decision process considered here) is correctly specified; see Rust (1994d), p. 3086. I discuss this issue next.

Methodological issues and the identification of MDPs

As noted before, structural models of intertemporal decisions are based on the maintained assumption that agents are rational expected-utility maximizers. The mathematical models that correspond to this view of economic decisions such as Markov decision processes are relatively complicated when compared to models of static decisions. The mathematical apparatus used surely provokes some methodological questions (see, *inter alia*, Burtless (1989) and Pemberton (1993) for discussions). Does it make any sense to suggest that agents solve intertemporal optimization problems which take hours to be solved numerically on a supercomputer? Or to argue that agents behave *as if* they were solving a complicated mathematical problem, following Friedman (1953)? Also, experimental studies have shown that some of the assumptions underlying the neoclassical theory of intertemporal decision-making are systematically violated. For example, experimental studies have found that people discount the distant future more heavily than implicit in the assumption of exponential discounting (see Camerer (1995), pp. 649–651).

Rust (1994a) has considered these objections extensively. He argues that the usefulness of the structural approach is primarily an empirical issue, and he provides an extensive overview of empirical applications of both continuous and discrete Markov decision processes. He comes to the conclusion that the empirical performance of discrete MDP models is encouraging when they are judged by their ability to rationalize individual decisions (within a methodological *as if* framework). However, continuous MDP models applied to macro data have consistently been rejected, a fact that Rust attributes primarily to aggregation problems, and continuous MDP models applied to micro data (such as Euler-equation based investment models, see Section 2.1) have had mixed success, a fact that has been partially attributed to poor small-sample properties of the GMM estimators involved. Generally, there seems to be a trend towards the specification of discrete MDP models for very specific economic problems where suitable microdata are available. In the case of firms' decisions, such data are available in plant-level datasets such as the Longitudinal Research Database used in this study.

There is another methodological problem that arises when an intertemporal model of economic decisions is applied to real-world phenomena: For structural estimation of an intertemporal optimization model, the researcher needs to make strong *a priori* identifying assumptions. Such assumptions reflect the fact that without any further restrictions, the dynamic programming framework itself has no empirically testable implication – it just imposes the assumption of intertemporal optimization and rational expectations on the agents (see Rust (1994d)). Therefore, the researcher needs to impose *a priori* identifying restrictions on the model (i. e., on the utility function, $u(\cdot)$, and on the state transition matrix, $p(\cdot)$, taking the form of parametric specifications). Because of such assumptions, however, the researcher also needs to thorougly test any structural model. Rust (1994d), p. 3115, notes: "One has an obligation to go beyond simply reporting parameter estimates and their standard errors." Tests of structural models can take the form of either in-sample specification tests, or out-of-sample predictive tests (although the latter are sometimes difficult to perform due to the typically short spells of data available for many problems). Examples of test procedures in a structural DDP model are discussed in Section 3.2.3.

An alternative approach to theory-guided empirical research in economics that has received much interest in recent years is to "eschew theory in favor of a 'data should speak for themselves' view" (Keane and Wolpin (1997), p. 112). This approach would have empirical research rely on either randomized social experiments or on natural experiments from which inference can be drawn about the effects of, say, an economic policy intervention (a "treatment") without having to rely on economic theory or having to make strong auxiliary assumptions. But, as Keane and Wolpin state, "although experiments can tell us what happend to a particular population at a particular time for a specific treatment, to generalize to other contexts requires that we learn about the mechanism generating the response" (p. 112).

To summarize the methodological issues raised here, it is my view that the theoretical appeal of intertemporal optimization models in general, and of the flexibility of the Markov decision process framework considered here, justify at least trying to specify and estimate comprehensive structural models of intertemporal choice. Even if such models are considered unrealistic, they might well allow for accurate out-of-sample predictions and hence facilitate the simulation of the effects of proposed policy changes. Also, even if one gives up the assumptions of maximizing behavior and rational expectations, this framework can still be used as a benchmark for evaluating alternative models. For example, one can assess the empirical implications of alternative models in which agents use a non-optimizing strategy (such as rules of thumb) by the loss in utility or profit that they suffer relative to optimal behavior (given by the solution to the intertemporal optimization problem). To conduct such a comparison, the researcher needs to solve the intertemporal optimization problem in any case, even if real-world agents do not. A deeper understanding of intertemporal optimization models and their empirical implications is still called for; this is particularly true for models that involve non-standard constraints, as discussed in Chapter 2 and Section 3.1.4.

Structural estimation and policy simulation: two examples

To conclude this section, I sketch two examples of successful structural estimation of discrete decision processes; these models illustrate the advantages of the structrual approach for performing policy simulations in applied work.

One area in which structural methods have been widely used is the analysis of retirement decisions; examples include Berkovec and Stern (1991) and Blau (1994). Lumsdaine *et al.* (1992) compare the empirical performance of various reduced-form and structural models of retirement decisions. However, they stop short of actually estimating a full structural model of retirement decisions that would correspond to the framework presented in Section 3.1. Such an approach has been suggested by Rust (1989), and only recently have first results become available with the study of Rust and Phelan (1997). They investigate retirement decisions in the presence of various distorting regulations of the U.S. Social Security and Medicare systems and of incomplete markets for loans, annuities, and health insurance. This paper contains the most complete MDP model of retirement behavior ever estimated with structural methods. In particular, the model places no restrictions on labor supply paths (i. e., retirement is not assumed to be an absorbing state), and separates the labor supply decision from the retirement (i. e., social security acceptance) decision; hence, the model has two discrete control variables. In many respects, I follow Rust and Phelan's modelling strategy in the model of joint investment and exit decisions presented in Section 3.3.

Another example for the usefulness of structural approaches in the evaluation of policy changes is a series of papers by Rust and Rothwell on operating decisions for U.S. nuclear power plants (NPPs).[41] Using a unique dataset with monthly operating histories for all 116 NPPs that where in operation in the U.S. over the 1975–93 period, they simulate the effects of changes in safety regulations (caused mainly by the Three Mile Island accident in March 1979). The recursive decision problem solved by the electric utility's managers running a NPP is whether and at what level of capacity to operate the reactor, to shut it down for refueling or preventive maintenance, or to permanently close the plant. These decision variables are either discrete in nature, or are appropriately discretized (in the case of operating capacity). The state variables include the reactor's age, the length of the last refueling spell and the observed operating status. The central trade-off faced by plant managers is between cost efficiency (determined *inter alia* by forced unplanned outages), fuel efficiency and plant safety, and this trade-off seems to be picked up well by the DDP model.

Other applications of MDP methods in structural econometric studies include a study by Das (1992) on operating decisions for cement kilns,

[41] See Rust and Rothwell (1995) and Rothwell and Rust (1995, 1997).

by Pakes (1986) on optimal patent renewal, by Wolpin (1984) on fertility decisions, and by Montgomery (1991) on migration decisions in rural Malaysia. I will discuss the econometric techniques used in these models in the next section.

3.2.2 Structural estimation of Markov decision processes

There are two major approaches to the structural estimation of Markov decision processes. The first approach deals with cases in which closed-form solutions for the underlying optimization problem exist; this is the case for the class of continuous (and mixed discrete-continuous) Markov decision processes that have Euler equations derived from first-order conditions. From the Euler equation, moment restrictions can be derived, and estimation can be performed by the generalized method of moments (GMM) estimator (Hansen (1982) and Hansen and Singleton (1982)). I do not discuss GMM estimation here; see Hall (1993) and Ogaki (1993) for recent reviews of the theory and applications.

The second approach concentrates on the case where no closed-form solutions exist, which is the case for most DDP and some CDP models; the framework used is that of full information maximum likelihood (FIML) estimation. In such algorithms, a dynamic programming problem (or some other nonlinear dynamic optimization problem) is solved numerically for given values of the parameters in an inner loop. This solution is then nested in an outer loop to find the optimal parameters in a maximum likelihood framework. The idea of estimating nonlinear rational expectations models by FIML methods has first been explored by Fair and Taylor (1983); their approach, in turn, extends the analysis of ML estimation in the linear-quadratic case (in which an explicit solution for the underlying optimization problem exists) pioneered by Hansen and Sargent (1980, 1981). For a recent review of this approach, see Fair (1996).

In the following, I concentrate on econometric methods for discrete and mixed discrete-continuous dynamic models; I also discuss methods for models with explicit (market) interactions between agents. Mostly, these methods belong to the full-information maximum likelihood methods.

Discrete decision processes

Structural estimation methods for discrete decision processes are fundamentally different from the Euler equation methods that are available for continuous decision processes. Since the control variable is discrete, the objective function cannot be differentiated to derive a first-order condition. There are various approaches to circumvent this difficulty; they are mainly based on methods developed for the estimation of static discrete-choice models. As Section 3.2.3 is devoted entirely to Rust's (1987, 1988) nested fixed-point algorithm (NFXP) which constitutes a leading example of a full information maximum likelihood estimator for DDPs, the discussion here concentrates on the general structure of DDP estimation. Rust (1994d) provides further details.

In the econometric analysis of static discrete-choice models, an agent's choices are assumed to be governed by the relative magnitude of the single period utility function $u(\cdot, \theta_u)$ across available alternatives, and the parameter vector θ_u is estimated by maximum likelihood. In dynamic models of discrete choice, the agents' choices depend on the value function V whose functional form is generally not known even if the single-period utility function u is. Agents' choices also depend on their beliefs about the stochastic evolution of state variables (summarized in the state transition density $p(\cdot, \theta_p)$), and on their discount rate, β. Hence the parameter vector is given by $\theta = (\theta_u, \theta_p, \beta)$.

The maximum likelihood approach to a dynamic discrete-choice model is to compute the best fitting estimate of θ by repeatedly solving for the unknown value function V for each trial value of θ. This method, known as the nested fixed-point algorithm (NFXP), has been developed by John Rust (1987, 1988). As discussed in Section 3.2.3 below, this nested numerical solution approach requires a number of arguably strong assumptions in the underlying behavioral framework. These assumptions are, *inter alia*, an additively separable decomposition of the utility function into observed components and an error term, and a conditional independence assumption for the state transition density. These assumptions have been used widely in the literature on static discrete-choice models and hence are not specific to the structural estimation of *dynamic* discrete-choice models.

While the assumptions of additive separability and conditional independence might seem unsatisfactory in certain applications, the virtue of this framework is its generality: In principle, the parameters of any discrete decision process formulated in the general structure of Section 3.1 can be estimated by the nested fixed-point algorithm, although the computational burden of repeatedly solving the value function to find the best-fitting parameter vector effectively introduces an upper bound for the number of decision and state variables that can be considered in practice. However, this frontier is moving outward quite fast with the introduction of more efficient solution methods for DDPs, as discussed in Section 3.1.3, and with the increase in computing power that is available even in desktop computers.

There are a few approaches that relax the assumption of either additive separability or conditional independence. As Rust (1994d), p. 3118, notes, there is, however, no general theory for DDP estimation without these assumptions. Therefore, most of these alternative approaches are very specific to the empirical problem at hand, and mostly they apply to the finite-horizon case. The nested fixed-point framework, on the other hand, covers infinite-horizon DDPs and hence finite-horizon problems as a special case. For the latter, optimal policies can be computed by backward induction which avoids the numerically more demanding solution of the fixed-point problem that arises in the infinite-horizon case.

An interesting approach for the infinite-horizon case with a single discrete control variable is due to Hotz and Miller (1993); its main virtue is that it avoids the numerical solution of the fixed-point problem. The idea is to obtain consistent estimates of the conditional choice probabilities by focusing on a single "terminating" alternative that leads into an absorbing state, such as a woman's sterilisation decision or a firm's market exit decision in models of industry dynamics.[42] Given a parametric estimate of the value function for this alternative, the idea is to uncover the functional forms of the remaining alternatives non-parametrically by inverting a mapping from value functions into choice probabilities (such a mapping is derived below for the more general case of DDPs estimated with the nested fixed-point algorithm, see equation (3.15)). Once the

[42] However, this approach would not allow for more than one choice variable such as in the DDP model of firm investment considered in this study.

value function has been estimated for all alternatives, the parameters of interest can be estimated using partial maximum likelihood or generalized method of moments estimators. A related approach by Hotz *et al.* (1994) avoids parametric estimation of the value function for the terminating alternative by using Monte Carlo simulation and non-parametric estimation methods. See Rust (1994b), p. 151, for an introduction to these methods.

Mixed discrete-continuous models

In Section 3.3.1, I will present a model of firm's joint investment and exit decisions with mixed discrete-continuous control variables. A similar structure can be found in a model of an individual's joint savings and retirement decisions and many other economic applications. Some examples follow below; see also Pudney (1989), pp. 131–136, for an overview. Mixed discrete-continuous models represent an interesting case on the borderline of continuous and discrete Markov decision models. Not surprisingly, there are attempts to extend the estimation methods developed for either framework to the mixed discrete-continuous case.

As described before, continuous decision processes whose optimal decision rules can be expressed in terms of a stochastic Euler equation are amenable to structural estimation using the generalized method of moments (GMM) estimator. Construction of the Euler equation, however, requires differentiation with respect to the control variable a, hence it is not immediately clear whether similar techniques can be used for mixed-discrete decision processes where a has discrete components (while it is clear that such methods cannot be used for pure discrete decision processes).

Pakes (1994) shows how a stochastic Euler equation (similar to (3.8)) can be derived from relatively simple mixed discrete-continuous models (such as the model of Section 3.3.1 without financial constraints). In the next step, one can construct moment conditions which allow structural estimation with a GMM-type method. However, the ability to construct GMM estimators is lost if there are additional constraints that bind only occasionally, such as the cases of irreversibility and financial constraints discussed in Section 3.1.4.

This latter point was one of the reasons for why I decided to use a pure DDP framework this study: Incorporating further restrictions seems to be easier. The DDP approach to the estimation of mixed discrete-continuous models has been developed, *inter alia*, by Vassilis Hajivassiliou and John Rust. Recall from the discussion of theoretical solutions for such models in Section 3.1.4 that the central idea of this approach is to concentrate on discrete choices that correspond to the underlying continuous choice. While approximating continuous decision variables with discrete decisions might seem crude at first sight, empirical applications work quite well because the expected utility pay-offs associated with these discrete choices can still be modelled realistically.

In a string of papers, Hajivassiliou and Ioannides (1994), Corres *et al.* (1997), and Corres and Ioannides (1994) have applied this approach to households' consumption and labor supply decisions, to firms' investment and financing decisions, and to firms' investment and exit decisions, respectively; econometric estimation is performed using dynamic reduced-form methods in these papers (in particular, they use the simulated maximum likelihood estimator by Börsch-Supan and Hajivassiliou (1993)). The papers by Rust and his co-authors, in contrast, use the nested fixed-point framework for structural estimation of the DDPs derived from the underlying mixed-discrete decision processes. Some examples will serve to illustrate the structural approach.

In the empirical study of nuclear power plant (NPP) operation mentioned earlier, Rothwell and Rust (1997) replace the discrete choices (whether to permanently close, refuel, or operate the power plant) and the continuous choice of the capacity at which the plant is run (which is bounded between 0 and 1, corresponding to shutting down the plant temporarily and running at full capacity) by a single discrete variable that takes 8 different values:

$a_t = 1$	permanently close the NPP
$a_t = 2$	refuel the NPP
$a_t = 3$	shut down the NPP (i. e., run the NPP at 0 % capacity)
$a_t = 4$	run the NPP at between 1 % and 25 % capacity
$a_t = 5$	run the NPP at between 26 % and 50 % capacity
$a_t = 6$	run the NPP at between 51 % and 75 % capacity
$a_t = 7$	run the NPP at between 76 % and 99 % capacity
$a_t = 8$	run the NPP at 100 % capacity

An interesting feature of the model is the way in which the choice set, $A_t(s_t)$, depends on the current state: Not all values of a_t can be chosen in every period, i. e., they depend on the operation status of the plant.

Rust and Phelan (1997) present a DDP model of joint labor supply and social security acceptance decisions for U.S. males. Here, the labor supply decision has some continuous aspects, although it might seem quite natural to approximate this decision by a discrete variable, given various institutional restrictions on labor supply (i. e., on hours worked). The model has two discrete decision variables, a_t^1 and a_t^2.

$a_t^1 = 1$ if the individual is not employed
$a_t^1 = 2$ if the individual is half-time employed
$a_t^1 = 3$ if the individual is full-time employed
$a_t^2 = 0$ if the individual does not apply for social security benefits
$a_t^2 = 1$ if the individual applies for social security benefits

In the mixed discrete-continuous model of plant-level investment and exit decisions I present in Section 3.3.1, the control variables, operating status and investment, take the following values:

$\chi_t = 1$ if the plant is active during period t
$\chi_t = 0$ if the plant is closed or sold during period t
$i_t \in (-(1-\delta)k, \bar{\imath})$ continuous investment choice in period t

Note that, in practice, the continuous control variable needs to be discretized. Also, the investment variable is bounded below by the negative of the existing capital stock and above by some arbitrary (large) value $\bar{\imath} < \infty$. I return to these issues below.

Market interactions and endogenous market structure

The empirical model used in this study analyzes firm behavior in a pure decision-theoretic context; essentially, the firm's decisions can be viewed as playing a game against nature. However, some exogenous variables that form part of the firm's decision making process reflect market equilibrium outcomes: The evolution of output prices, for example, reflects both macroeconomic shocks and the competitive nature of the industry. The exit rule derived from an investment model with endogenous exit decisions therefore implicitly reflects market interactions.

In general, it is possible to explicitly model the role of market interactions for firms' investment and exit decisions; Section 2.1 provided a discussion of theoretical models along these lines. I conclude this section with a brief review of econometric techniques that have recently been developed to address this issue in empirical work. Just like the structural estimation of dynamic discrete-choice models, this is currently a very active area of econometric frontier research; also, empirical applications are still quite rare. Pakes (1994), pp. 217–243, provides an overview of structural estimation methods for models with market interactions.

The structural econometric models discussed here are based on the theoretical framework of Markov-perfect industry dynamics by Ericson and Pakes (1995). It focuses on the impact of uncertainty that arises from investment in research and exploration-type processes and derives investment and exit rules for incumbent firms. Then, it adds an entry rule and finally aggregates the optimal behavior of all firms, including potential entrants, into a rational expectations, Markov-perfect industry equilibrium.

In the formal framework of Markov decision processes considered in this study, such a model implies that the returns an agent earns in a given period depend not only on the value of the agent's own state vector, $\tilde{s}_t$, but also on the vector of state variables of all other agents active in the market, $\hat{s}_t$. Assuming that there is an upper bound on the number of agents active in a market, the industry structure is a finite list of the state vectors of all agents, $s = (\hat{s}, \tilde{s})$. The agent's actions depend on the vector $(\hat{s}, \tilde{s})$, but not on other variables such as past actions. In the industrial organization literature, the related theoretical concept is known as Markov-perfect Nash equilibrium. The first step to make this framework amenable to empirical analysis is to derive algorithms that allow solving the industry equilibrium for a (relatively) large number of market participants. Such algorithms have been constructed by Pakes and McGuire (1994, 1995, 1996).[43] As in other applications of Markov decision processes, the central problem of such algorithms is the numerical burden associated with computing the expectation of future states (i. e., multivariate integrals), and the fact that these models have high-dimensional

[43] Pakes *et al.* (1993) discuss the implementation of such algorithms in the Gauss and C programming languages and provide sample code.

state vectors only exacerbates the problems involved. Similar to new approaches for solving DDP models with large state spaces, the most recent paper, Pakes and McGuire (1996), uses Monte Carlo techniques to compute these integrals. The authors note that their algorithm is several orders of magnitudes faster than earlier versions.

Given a numerical solution of the market equilibrium, the econometric estimation of such models could, in principle, be performed using a nested maximum likelihood approach such as Rust's NFXP algorithm: The parameters of the model would then be estimated by solving for the complete set of dynamic equilibrium responses for different candidate values of the parameter vector, and then nesting these in an iterative maximum likelihood procedure. As Pakes (1994), p. 219, notes, the computational and data requirements for such an approach are unlikely to be satisfied in the near future. The alternative approach followed by Pakes and other authors in this literature is to break the estimation problem into smaller parts: "Each part should allow the researcher to obtain an estimator for a subvector of the total vector of the model's parameters. This vector should be obtainable without having to solve for the complete set of equilibrium responses, but should be consistent and asymptotically normal under the *complete* set of equilibrium assumptions." (*ibid.*)

An example for this approach is the study of investment and exit dynamics in the U.S. telecommunications equipment industry by Olley and Pakes (1996). The model builds on a Cobb-Douglas production function. Note that estimating this relationship by OLS would introduce biases caused by the endogeneity of input demands in the presence of stochastic shocks to productivity, and by the self-selection induced by endogenous exit behavior. The approach chosen by Olley and Pakes is to break up the estimation problem in smaller parts. Ultimately, the production function is estimated by semiparametric methods. In particular, they use a partially linear model with a single variable factor, labor, and a function of the quasi-fixed factors (plant age and capital) and an unobserved state variable (productivity). The estimation of the parameters of the quasi-fixed factors, in turn, requires estimation of survival probabilities. The properties of the resulting semiparametric estimator have been analyzed by Pakes and Olley (1995).

A brief assessment of structural econometric methods for MDPs

Given the current state of research in this field, there seems to be a trade-off between a framework that allows for additional restrictions on households' or firms' individual decisions (such as irreversibilities or financial constraints) and a framework that allows for market interactions between agents. Each of these extensions to the standard MDP framework has its theoretical appeal, but also increases the computational burden associated with the numerical solution of the intertemporal optimization problem. At some later stage of this research program, it might be possible to incorporate both kinds of extensions to the standard MDP model of, say, firm behavior in a unifying empirical framework, but the computational burden of such endeavors is likely to remain a major obstacle for some time. In empirical applications, it is therefore necessary to make strong assumptions about the behavior of economic agents, and any application is likely to leave out some aspect that would be interesting from a theoretical view.

3.2.3 The nested fixed-point algorithm

The nested fixed-point algorithm (NFXP) used in this study for the econometric analysis of the controlled mixed discrete-continuous process that governs firms' investment and exit decisions was developed, and first applied in an empirical study, by John Rust (1987, 1988). This section contains a brief overview of the algorithm's underlying behavioral assumptions, of the maximum likelihood framework used for estimation, and of its asymptotic properties and methods for hypothesis testing.

Intertemporal optimization and models of the error term

When Markov decision processes are estimated structurally, a fundamental problem arises: The optimal decision rule $\alpha(s)$ is, according to Blackwell's theorem stated earlier, a *deterministic* function of the agent's state, s. As Rust (1994d), p. 3100, notes, it is, however, not conceivable that any theory will be able to predict human behavior perfectly. Therefore, there will be discrepancies between the predictions of any MDP model (or any other model of human behavior, for that matter) and observed behavior. The problem, then, is to find a suitable interpretation of this discrepancy, or, in Rust's words, a "model of the error term". Rust discusses four alternatives:

- optimization errors;
- measurement errors;
- approximation errors;
- unobserved state variables.

The view taken in the behavioral set-up of Rust's nested fixed-point algorithm is that errors are related to unobserved state variables, so I concentrate on this approach below. Here are some brief remarks on the other views (taken from Rust (1994d), pp. 3100–3101).

Optimization errors The optimization error model implies that an agent who "intends" to behave according to the optimal decision rule $\alpha(s)$ takes an actual decision that deviates from $\alpha(s)$ by an optimization error. Rust argues that such a discrepancy between actual and optimal decisions is logically inconsistent: If the agent knew that there are random factors that lead to *ex post* discrepancies between intended and realized actions, he would re-optimize to take these uncertainties into account. If, on the other hand, the error is interpreted as accounting for irrational or non-maximizing behavior, it is not clear why this behavior should take the form of random deviations from the rational decision rule $\alpha(s)$ (as the agent would have to know this rule in order to give deviations from it any meaning).

Measurement errors In empirical work, measurement errors are commonplace. Rust notes that they are more likely to occur in continuous components of the state vector than in discrete components of the decision vector, but classification errors for discrete-choice variables are possible, too. Measurement errors in the state variables are important because the optimal policy $\alpha(s)$ is typically a non-linear function of the state s. There is as yet no general theory of measurement errors in non-linear models; only in special cases can measurement errors be accounted for in structural models of dynamic choice (e. g., Eckstein and Wolpin (1989)).

Approximation errors In the MDP framework, an approximation error is the difference between actual observed behavior and the optimal decision implied by the solution to the MDP model. As mentioned earlier, every MDP model will be misspecified in the sense that it cannot predict economic behavior perfectly, so approximation errors are bound to occur. In this view, the econometric problem is to find a specification of the agent's primitives $(u(\cdot), p(\cdot), \beta)$ that minimizes the approximation error according to some metric. Rust argues that this approach leads to "degenerate" econometric estimators with poor asymptotic properties; also, the choice of an appropriate metric to determine whether a given model provides a good approximation relative to observed behavior is difficult.

The behavioral framework with unobserved state variables

Assume that the vector of state variables, s, can be partitioned in two components, a vector of state variables, x, that can be observed by both the optimizing agent and the econometrician, and a vector of unobserved state variables, ϵ, which are known to the agent but cannot be observed by the econometrician. Hence, $s = (x, \epsilon)$, and the optimal decision rule is given by $\alpha(x, \epsilon)$. Given that the specification of the unobserved components is rich enough, any observed behavior can be rationalized as an optimal (deterministic) action given *some* value for ϵ.

Given this set-up, the parameters of interest can be estimated using a maximum likelihood approach based on the conditional choice probabilities,

$$P(a|x, \theta) = \int I(a = \alpha(x, \epsilon, \theta))q(\mathrm{d}\epsilon|x)\,, \tag{3.15}$$

where $q(\mathrm{d}\epsilon|x)$ is the conditional distribution of the unobserved components, ϵ, given the observed state variables, x; $\alpha(\cdot)$ is the optimal policy functon; and $I(\cdot)$ is the indicator function. The next section focuses on how these conditional choice probabilities can be specified and estimated.

The econometric estimation of dynamic discrete decision processes with maximum likelihood methods requires two assumptions about the agent's utility function and state transition density: additive separability and conditional independence, respectively. These assumptions ensure a saturated specification for the unobservables in the DDP model; they are borrowed from the literature on static discrete models (see McFadden

(1981)). A saturated specification implies that the conditional choice probabilities have full support (technically, $a \in A(x) \iff P(a|x) > 0$), i. e., there is a positive probability of observing any possible choice in the sample. Naturally, estimation of the likelihood function would be impossible if such zero probability choices were encountered in the sample.

Assumption AS: Additive separability (see Rust (1994d), p. 3102)

The choice set depends only on the observed variable, x, $A(s) = A(x)$. The unobserved state variable, ϵ, is a vector with at least as many components as the number of elements in $A(x)$. The utility function has the additively separable decomposition

$$u(s,a) = u(x,a) + \epsilon(a) .$$

Assumption CI: Conditional independence (see Rust (1994d), p. 3103)

The transition density for the controlled Markov process $\{x_t, \epsilon_t\}$ can be factored as

$$p(\mathrm{d}x_{t+1}, \mathrm{d}\epsilon_{t+1}|x_t, a_t, \epsilon_t) = q(\mathrm{d}\epsilon_{t+1}|x_{t+1})\pi(\mathrm{d}x_{t+1}|x_t, a_t) .$$

The conditional independence assumption requires some explanation. Essentially, this assumption implies that the error process $\{\epsilon_t\}$ is a noise process independent of the main dynamics of the model which are reflected in the transition probability $\pi(\mathrm{d}x_{t+1}|x_t, a_t)$. In particular,

- x_{t+1} is a sufficient statistic for ϵ_{t+1}, i. e., any serial dependence between the error terms is transmitted entirely through the observed state variable x_{t+1}, or, $\{\epsilon_t\}$ is an i.i.d. process independent of the *current* state, s_t;
- the probability density for next period's state, x_{t+1}, depends only on the current state, x_t, and not on the current error, ϵ_t.

Under assumptions AS and CI, the empirical Bellman equation for the general DDP problem derived in Section 3.1 can be written as follows:

$$\begin{aligned} V_\theta(x,\epsilon) &= \max_{a \in A(x)} \left[v(x,a,\theta) + \epsilon(a) \right], \quad \text{where} \qquad (3.16) \\ v(x,a,\theta) &= u(x,a,\theta_u) + \beta \int V_\theta(x',\epsilon) q(\mathrm{d}\epsilon|x')\pi(\mathrm{d}x'|x,a,\theta_p) . \end{aligned}$$

The structure of this DDP problem is the same as in the static discrete-choice problem, but the value function $v(\cdot)$ replaces the single-period utility function $u(\cdot)$. Rust (1994d), p. 3104, uses these assumptions to define the empirical discrete decision process that underlies his maximum likelihood estimation approach; this definition is given in Table 3.3. Note that this empirical DDP is a special case of the Markov decision process summarized in Table 3.1, so all results derived for general MDPs apply to the empirical DDP as well.

Table 3.3: The empirical discrete Markov decision process

- A discrete time index, $t \in \{0, 1, 2, \ldots, T\}, T \leq \infty$.
- A state space, S, defined as the product space $S = X \times E$, where X is a Borel subset of $\mathbb{R}^J$ and $E = \mathbb{R}^{|A|}$.
- A decision (action) space, $A = \{1, \ldots, \sup_{s \in S}|A(s)|\}$.
- A family of constraint sets, $A(s) = A(x) \subseteq A$ for all $s \in S$ and $x \in X$.
- A (Markov) transition probability $p(\mathrm{d}s'|s, a)$ that satisfies assumption CI, and where the component $q(\mathrm{d}\epsilon|x)$ of the transition probability is a product measure on $\mathbb{R}^{|A(x)|} \times \mathbb{R}^{|A|-|A(x)|}$ whose first component has support $\mathbb{R}^{|A(x)|}$ and whose second component is a unit mass on a vector of zeroes of length $|A| - |A(x)|$.
- A single period utility function $u(s_t, a_t)$ that satisfies assumption AS.
- A discount factor $\beta \in [0, 1)$.
- A utility functional with additively separable decomposition, $U(s, a) = \sum_{t=0}^{T} \beta^{-t} u(s_t, a_t)$.

Source: Adapted from Rust (1994d), p. 3104.

The dynamic multinomial logit model and ML estimation

Given the assumptions stated in Table 3.3, the conditional choice probability (3.15) can be written as the partial derivative of the *social surplus function*[44] $G(\cdot)$ with respect to $u(\cdot)$:

$$P(a|x) = \frac{\partial G[\{u(x, a), a \in A(x)\}|x]}{\partial u(x, a)}, \quad \text{where} \tag{3.17}$$

$$G[\{u(x, a), a \in A(x)\}|x] = \int \max_{a \in A(x)} [u(x, a) + \epsilon(a)] q(\mathrm{d}\epsilon|x). \tag{3.18}$$

44 The social surplus function has been introduced in the literature on static discrete-choice models by McFadden (1981).

Note that the integral in (3.18) has dimension $|A|$. This result (Rust (1994d), p. 3104) is a central component of the maximum likelihood estimator that forms the outer loop of the nested fixed-point algorithm, again replacing $u(\cdot)$ by the value function $v(\cdot)$.

Further, Rust (1988) has proved that under the assumptions made so far, in particular if the underlying process of state and decision variables, $\{s_t, a_t\}$, is an empirical DDP defined in Table 3.3, then the *observed* components, $\{x_t, a_t\}$, follow a controlled Markov process with transition probability given by

$$\text{Prob}(\mathrm{d}x', a'|x, a) = P(a'|x') \cdot \pi(\mathrm{d}x'|x, a)\,. \tag{3.19}$$

Next, certain functional form assumptions have to be made in order to construct the maximum likelihood estimator of the parameters that enter the DDP. Assume that the conditional distribution of the error term is multivariate extreme-value, i. e.,

$$q(\mathrm{d}\epsilon|x) = \prod_{a\in A(x)} \exp\{-\epsilon(a) + \gamma\}\exp[-\exp\{-\epsilon(a) + \gamma\}]\,, \tag{3.20}$$

where γ is a constant that insures that the extreme value distribution has unconditional mean zero. Then the conditional choice probabilities are given by multinomial logits,

$$P(a|x) = \frac{\exp\{v(x, a)\}}{\sum_{\tilde{a}\in A(x)} \exp\{v(x, \tilde{a})\}}\,. \tag{3.21}$$

In contrast to the static multinomial logit model, the utilities entering here are not single-period utilities, but are derived from the solution of the DDP problem: $v(\cdot)$ is the fixed point to the contraction mapping

$$\begin{aligned}\Gamma(v)(x, a) &= u(x, a) \\ &\quad + \beta \int \log\left(\sum_{a'\in A(x)} \exp\{v(x, a')\}\right)\pi(\mathrm{d}x'|x, a)\,. \end{aligned} \tag{3.22}$$

While the static multinomial logit model implies the – in many respects undesirable – property of independence from irrelevant alternatives (IIA), the logit formulation derived from the intertemporal DDP model does not: From (3.22), one can see that any choice generally depends on the attributes of all other alternatives even when the single-period utility only depends on the utility of the chosen alternative. As Rust (1994d) stresses, this implies that while the extreme-value specification chosen here yields the computational simplifications associated with the existence of closed-form expressions for $P(\cdot)$ and $G(\cdot)$, it avoids the disadvantage of having an IIA property.

Using the specifications just derived, the full information maximum likelihood estimator for the N parameters of interest is defined by

$$\hat{\theta} = \arg\max_{\theta \in \mathbb{R}^N} L(\theta) = \prod_{i=1}^{I} \prod_{t=t_1^i}^{t_T^i} P(a_t^i | x_t^i, \theta) \pi(\mathrm{d}x_t^i | x_{t-1}^i, a_{t-1}^i, \theta) . \quad (3.23)$$

for (unbalanced) panel data $\{x_t^i, a_t^i\}$.

The main complication of the maximum likelihood framework derived so far is that while the conditional choice probabilities have a closed-form solution, this solution is in terms of the optimized value function. The latter is, in general, not known but has to be solved numerically (e. g., by one of the methods discussed in Section 3.1). This leads to Rust's (1987, 1988) nested fixed-point algorithm for estimating the parameter vector θ. The structure of this algorithm with its nested loops is depicted in Figure 3.1. The main steps of this algorithm are:

- In an "inner" loop, use a contraction fixed-point algorithm to compute v_θ for each trial value of θ.
- In an "outer" hill-climbing algorithm, search for the value of θ that solves (3.23), the maximum likelihood estimator $\hat{\theta}$.

The facts that the partial derivative of the value function v_θ exists and that it is a continuous function of θ imply that the outer loop of the algorithm can use more efficient quasi-Newton gradient optimization methods. This derivative is given by

$$\frac{\partial v_\theta}{\partial \theta} = [I - \Gamma'_\theta(v)]^{-1} \left[\frac{\partial \Gamma'_\theta(v)}{\partial \theta} \right] \Bigg|_{v=v_\theta} . \quad (3.24)$$

As second derivatives are harder to compute, the BHHH algorithm (see Berndt *et al.* (1974)) is used because it requires only first derivates, approximating the negative of the Hessian of $L(\cdot)$ by the information matrix.

There is also a two-stage variant of the maximum likelihood estimator $\hat{\theta}$. Here, the parameter vector is partitioned into two components, $\theta = (\theta_1, \theta_2)$, where θ_1 are the parameters that appear only in the state

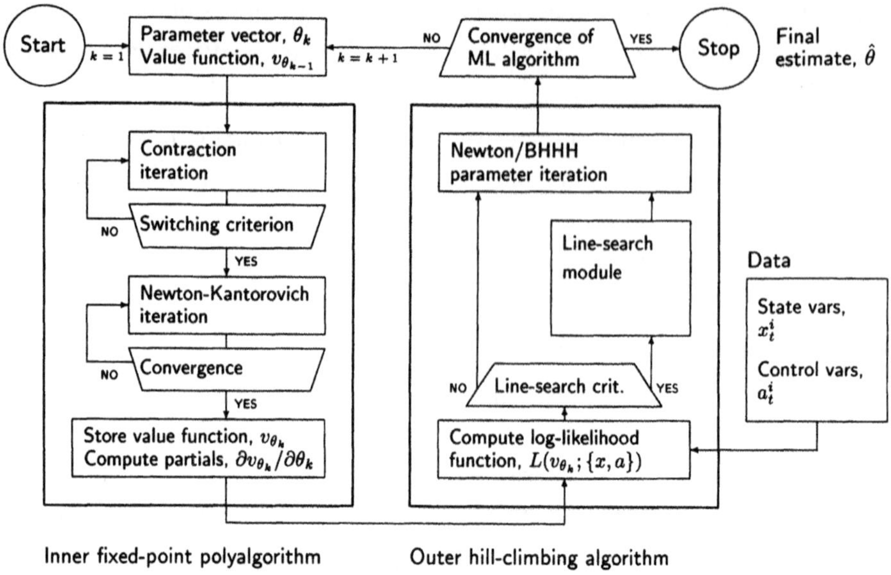

Figure 3.1: The nested fixed-point maximum likelihood algorithm
Source: Adapted from Rust (1988), p. 1017.

transition matrix $\pi(\cdot)$, while $\theta_2 = (\theta_u, \theta_q, \beta)$; this is admissible because the process of observed variables can be factored accordingly, see equation (3.19).

The first-stage estimator is the partial likelihood estimator

$$\hat{\theta}_1 = \underset{\theta_1 \in \mathbb{R}^{N_1}}{\arg\max}\ L_1(\theta_1) = \prod_{i=1}^{I} \prod_{t=t_1^i}^{t_T^i} \pi(\mathrm{d}x_t^i | x_{t-1}^i, a_{t-1}^i, \theta_1)\,. \tag{3.25}$$

Note that the estimation of θ_1 does not require a nested fixed-point algorithm to solve the DDP problem. The second-stage estimator takes the first-stage parameters of the state transition probability, $\hat{\theta}_1$, as given; it is defined as the partial likelihood estimator

$$\hat{\theta}_2 = \underset{\theta_2 \in \mathbb{R}^{N_2}}{\arg\max}\ L_2(\theta_2) = \prod_{i=1}^{I} \prod_{t=t_1^i}^{t_T^i} P(a_t^i | x_t^i, \hat{\theta}_1, \theta_2)\,. \tag{3.26}$$

The two-stage estimation method yields consistent, asymptotically normal, but inefficient estimates of the parameter vector θ. Its main advantage is that the number of parameters that are estimated in each stage is smaller than in the full information maximum likelihood estimator (3.23). This leads to considerable computational savings in the ML optimization procedure (in terms of the numbers of iterations typically required). This is particularly important in the case of the nested fixed-point algorithm where the DDP problem has to be solved repeatedly for each evaluation of the likelihood function.

Asymptotic properties of the NFXP estimator and formal tests

To derive the asymptotic properties of the NFXP estimator, a number of further assumptions have to be made regarding the sampling process of the panel data $\{x_t^i, a_t^i\}$ used for estimation. Rust (1994d), pp. 3111–3112, discusses these in detail. Here, I focus on the economic implication of an additional conditional independence assumption that allows for macroeconomic shocks (because this case is of particular relevance for empirical applications).

In general, deriving the asymptotic properties of the NFXP estimator could be based on the assumption that the realizations $\{x_t^i, a_t^i\}$ and $\{x_t^j, a_t^j\}$ are independent for different agents, $i \neq j$. However, this may not be plausible in models where all agents are affected by the same shocks; one can think of these as "macroeconomic" shocks. Examples include prices, interest rates, unemployment rates, news announcements, and many more. To allow for such shocks, partition the observed state variables into two (possibly vector-valued) components, a macroeconomic shock, m_t, that is common to all agents, and an idiosyncratic component, z_t, that is independently distributed across agents conditional on the realization of $\{m_t\}$.

Assumption CI-M: Conditional independence of macro shocks (see Rust (1994d), p. 3111)

The transition probability for the observed state variables, $x = (m, z)$, is given by

$$\pi(\mathrm{d}x'|x, a) = \pi_1(\mathrm{d}z'|z, m, a) \cdot \pi_2(\mathrm{d}m'|m) \,. \tag{3.27}$$

This assumption implies that macroeconomic shocks can affect the evolution of an agent's idiosyncratic (observed and unobserved) states $\{z_t^i\}$, but an individual's decision a_t^i has no effect on the evolution of the process $\{m_t\}$. This assumption seems reasonable when individual agents are small relative to the economy so that an individual's decision has no impact in the aggregate.

Theorem: Asymptotics of the NFXP maximum likelihood estimator (Rust (1988))

Under the set of assumptions stated in Rust (1994d), p. 3113, and under further regularity conditions stated in Rust (1988), the full information maximum likelihood estimator $\hat{\theta}$ (defined by (3.23)) has the following asymptotic properties:

1. $\hat{\theta}$ is a well-defined random variable;
2. $\hat{\theta}$ converges to the true value θ^* with probability 1 as the number of individuals in the panel tends to infinity, $I \longrightarrow \infty$;
3. the distribution of $\sqrt{I}(\hat{\theta} - \theta^*)$ converges weekly to $N(0, -H(\theta^*)^{-1})$, where $H(\theta^*)$ is the information matrix defined in Rust (1994d), p. 3113.

Note that a similar result can be obtained for the two-step partial likelihood version of the NFXP maximum likelihood estimator, see Rust (1994d), p. 3114.

In cases where the object of interest is the value function v_θ rather than the parameters θ, an additional asymptotic result is required. The estimated value function is required for policy simulations, for example, and in some cases confidence bands need to be computed. Such cases are covered by the following result. Note that the estimated value function $v_{\hat{\theta}}$ is a B-valued random element; i. e., an element of the Banach space $B(S)$ of all measurable, bounded functions (under the essential supremum norm) that map the state space onto the real line, $f : S \rightarrow I\!R$. Related measurability issues are covered by the assumptions stated by Rust (1988), p. 1012.

Theorem: Asymptotics of the estimated value function (Rust (1988))

Let $\hat{\theta}$ be a consistent estimator of θ^* with distribution $\sqrt{I}(\hat{\theta} - \theta^*)$ converging weekly to $N(0, -H(\theta^*)^{-1})$. Under the set of regularity conditions stated in Rust (1988),

1. $v_{\hat{\theta}}$ is a B-valued random element;

2. $v_{\hat{\theta}}$ converges weekly to v_{θ^*} with probability 1;

3. the distribution of $\sqrt{I}(v_{\hat{\theta}} - v_{\theta^*})$ converges to a Gaussian random element in B with vanishing expectation and covariance operator $\left[\frac{\partial v_{\theta^*}}{\partial \theta}\left(-H(\theta^*)^{-1}\right)\frac{\partial v_{\theta^*}}{\partial \theta'}\right]$.

Based on the asymptotic properties of the NFXP maximum likelihood estimator, hypothesis testing can use standard methods. For example, one might wish to test the conditional independence assumption CI. This assumption implies that the unobserved state variable ϵ_t is independent of ϵ_{t-1}, conditional on the value x_t of the observed state variable. This assumption can be tested by adding some function τ of the previous period control variables to the current period value function: $v_\theta(x_t, a_t) + \alpha\tau(a_{t-1})$. Under the null hypothesis that assumption CI is valid, the decision taken in period $t-1$ will have no effect on the decision taken in period t, conditional on the current state x_t; thus $\alpha = 0$ under the null hypothesis. Under the alternative, ϵ_t and ϵ_{t-1} will be serially correlated, even conditional on x_t, hence a_{t-1} will help predict a_t, and $\alpha \neq 0$. Either of the "holy trinity" tests (the Wald, likelihood ratio, or Lagrange multiplier tests) can be used for testing this hypothesis.

Another test that can be performed to test the overall specification of the DDP model is the chi-square goodness-of-fit test. Essentially, this is a joint test of two hypotheses: First, the maintained hypothesis that agents are rational, i. e., that they act *as if* their behavior were governed by an optimal decision rule implied by some DDP model, and second, that the particular functional forms chosen for $(u(\cdot), p(\cdot), \beta)$ by the econometrician are correct. However, the first assumption has no empirical content *per se*, due to the fundamental identification problem of Markov decision processes discussed above. The specification test hence provides a good way to diagnose specification errors. Unfortunately, there are some practical difficulties associated with this test, so it has rarely been used in practical applications so far; see Rust (1994d), pp. 3116–3118 for details.

3.3 An application: firms' joint investment and exit decisions

In this section, I present a dynamic programming model of firms' joint investment and market exit decisions. The theoretical tools I use are those developed in Section 3.1, and the model is formulated consistently with the empirical dynamic discrete-choice framework developed in Section 3.2.3. An empirical application of the model can be found in Chapter 4.

In Section 2.1.4, I argued that structural models of investment decisions require disaggregated data, and the empirical application of Chapter 4 uses a combination of plant and firm-level data. The basic idea is that firm headquarters make investment and production decisions for each plant independently, so that for each plant an intertemporal optimization problem must be solved. This interpretion is not required at this point, but for consistency, I use the terminology of plant-level production and investment decisions and firm-level financial situation throughout this section. The model could, in principle, be applied to firm-level investment decisions as well, so at this point this issue is purely one of terminology. However, as discussed in Section 2.1.4, it is an empirical question whether a structural model of investment decisions can be estimated successfully with more aggregated data such as, say, balance-sheet data recorded at the firm level.

3.3.1 Mixed discrete-continuous control variables

The following model of firms' intertemporal investment and exit decisions is formulated as a mixed discrete-continuous Markov decision process. For more details on this model, see Pakes (1994), pp. 175–200, on which this treatment is based.

In an intertemporal optimization model of firms' investment decisions, introducing endogenous market exit decisions (i. e., plant closure or sell-off) implies that the firm has an additional discrete control variable. At the beginning of each period, it can choose whether to continue operating *at all* or either to retire the plant or to sell it to some other firm.[45] Hence,

[45] It should be noted that plant sell-offs are of empirical relevance; for example, ownership changes are quite frequently observed in the LRD data used for estimation in

the firm's decision problem has two control variables, and the decision vector is given by $a = (\chi, i)$:

- a discrete control variable: continuation, χ_t, with
  $\chi_t = 1$ if the plant is active during period t, and
  $\chi_t = 0$ if the plant is closed or sold during period t;

- a continuous control variable: investment, i_t.

Firms are assumed to maximize the expected net present value of future returns, or cash flows, denoted by $\Pi(\cdot)$, for each plant individually. The objective function for a single plant is:

$$\max_{\alpha} E_{\alpha} \left\{ \sum_{t=0}^{\infty} \beta^t \Pi(s_t, a_t) | s_0 \right\} \tag{3.28}$$

where a_t is the vector of control variables, s_t is the vector of state variables, and $\alpha = \{a_0, a_1, a_2, \dots\}$ is a sequence of decisions (a policy).

Under some technical assumptions made by Pakes (1994), p. 176 (such as boundedness of the profit function and a discount rate bounded away from unity, an issue to which we return below), it can be shown that the optimal investment decision will never drive the capital stock to zero and will never reach some finite upper bound, $\bar{i}$. Hence, the firm's decision vector is given by

$$a = (\chi, i) \in A(s) = \{0, 1\} \times (-(1 - \delta)k, \bar{i}) , \tag{3.29}$$

where s is the vector of state variables in the current period. This formulation ensures that the optimal decision will never be at a corner of its choice set, $A(s)$. The state variables considered in this model can be derived from a model of industry dynamics such as Ericson and Pakes (1995): They include capital, k, and some stochastic shock variable ω.[46]

this project (see McGuckin and Nguyen (1995) and Section 4.A.1 for a discussion). Hence, the empirical model should try to incorporate both exit and ownership change decisions. For ease of exposition, the theoretical model discussed in this chapter is restricted to the binary choice whether to continue operation or not, but the extension is straightforward.

[46] Other state variables that one might wish to consider are plant age and the firm's financial status; these are being suppressed in the following for notational convenience.

The latter variable can also be interpreted as an unobserved state variable, and in practice one would need to specify some appropriate stochastic process for ω, such as a Markov transition density $p(d\omega'|\omega)$. The state vector is then given by:

$$s = (k, \omega) \in K \times \Omega \subset I\!R^2_+ \,. \tag{3.30}$$

Further, it is assumed that capital accumulation follows the standard law of motion, with δ being the depreciation rate,

$$k' = (1 - \delta)k + i \,. \tag{3.31}$$

Note that this formulation implies that investment is fully reversible by allowing gross investment to be negative. Finally, let $\tilde{k}$ be the scrap value of the plant's capital stock realized when the plant is closed down.[47]

The per-period profit function is, in general, given by

$$\Pi(s, a) = r(s, a) - c(s, a) \,, \tag{3.32}$$

where $r(\cdot)$ is per-period revenue (i.e., gross revenue, or, at the plant level, the value of shipments less operation and variable factor costs) and $c(\cdot)$ is the cost of adjusting the plant's capital stock according to the optimal decision rule. Note that (3.32) is a generalized version of the definition of the firm's cash flow used in Section 2.1.1 (equation (2.2)). Assuming that the decision to shut down the plant has no cost by itself and that capital stock adjustment costs depend only on investment, but not on the level of capital in place, this simplifies to $r(s, a) - c(i)$.[48]

The Bellman equation for the resulting mixed discrete-continuous control problem is given by:

$$V(s) = \sup_{a \in A(s)} \left[\Pi(s, a) + \beta \int V(s') p(ds'|s, a) \right] . \tag{3.33}$$

In this formulation, β is a time-invariant discount factor with $\beta \in [0, 1)$. In a general model of firm behavior, the discount factor would also have

47 The scrap value may not be equal to the current value of the capital stock; even $\tilde{k} = 0$ is possible.

48 The assumption that the cost function depends on investment is made for expositional convenience; as noted earlier, this is also the standard assumption in the investment literature. However, the argument can be extended for a cost function that depends both on investment and on the level of capital in place.

to reflect variations of interest rates over time and possibly states, but I defer a detailed discussion to Section 3.3.2.

Given the specifications above, the Bellman equation can be written as

$$\begin{aligned} V(k,\omega) &= \max_{\chi}\left\{\tilde{k}\,,\ \sup_{i}\left[r(s,a)-c(i)\right.\right. \\ &\qquad \left.\left. +\beta\int V(k',\omega')p(\mathrm{d}\omega'|\omega)\right]\right\}. \end{aligned} \tag{3.34}$$

Solving this problem yields a stochastic Euler equation similar to (3.8) which holds at the true values of the specified parameters. Pakes (1994) discusses how the standard Euler equation for continuous decision processes can be extended to the mixed discrete-continuous case by using variational arguments.

As discussed in Section 3.1.2, a number of technical assumptions are required to derive first-order conditions that characterize the solution to an intertemporal decision process. In particular, it is required that the per-period return function $r(s,a)$ is bounded, increasing in both its arguments, differentiable (with bounded derivative) and concave in k, and $\lim_{k\to 0}\frac{\partial r(\cdot)}{\partial k}=\infty$ and $\lim_{k\to\infty}\frac{\partial r(\cdot)}{\partial k}=0$, for all realizations of the unobserved component $\omega\in\Omega$. Further, assume that $c(i)$ is increasing, differentiable (with bounded derivative), and convex in i.

The resulting Euler equation can be written as:

$$\frac{\partial c(i)}{\partial i}=\beta\int\chi(s')\left\{\frac{\partial r(s')}{\partial k}+(1-\delta)\frac{\partial c(i(s'))}{\partial i}\right\}p(\mathrm{d}\omega'|\omega)\,. \tag{3.35}$$

The interpretation of this Euler equation is straightforward. It just says that the firm equates the marginal cost of investing another unit of capital this period and the expected marginal profit of such an investment in the following period. Note that in calculating next period's marginal profit, the firm takes into account its (expected) optimal continuation choice in the next period, $\chi(s')$. This argument illustrates the basic trade-off faced by a firm in a model with joint investment and exit decisions: The standard comparison of marginal cost and marginal benefit of investing into another unit of physical capital still holds, but the firm takes into account the optimal decision whether in the next period, any further production has positive net value at all.

The main advantage of this Euler equation is that the parameters of interest (such as those parameterizing the production and cost functions that enter $\Pi(\cdot)$) can be estimated by the generalized method of moments (GMM) approach; see Section 3.2 for details. This is due to the fact that in this particular case of a mixed discrete-continuous decision process there exists a closed-form solution to the maximization problem (3.33). The reason why this framework is not chosen in the subsequent analysis is that the ability to construct closed-form solutions is lost when further constraints, such as irreversibilities or financial constraints, are introduced.

In the empirical application presented in Chapter 4, I use the standard approach of the dynamic programming literature and discretize both the continuous choice variable, investment, and the corresponding continuous state variable, capital. The model is then solved by computing the optimal values of the control variables for each point of the discretized state space. Hence, the discretized version of the mixed discrete-continuous model of investment and exit decisions can be seen as a special case of the discrete decision process derived in Section 3.1.3, and this chapter's discussions of solving such a model and of the algorithm used for estimation apply.

The number of cells used to discretize the state space is determined by computational restrictions. Ideally, the number of cells should be large, as the numerical approximation to the solution is exact if the number of cells tends to infinity. In practice, the "curse of dimensionality" restricts the number of cells to the order of about 100. In this study, I used 100 cells during development and testing of the contraction algorithm that solves the (discretized version of the) mixed discrete-continuous model. In the actual estimation routine, where this solution forms the inner loop of the nested fixed-point algorithm, I used a somewhat coarser grid with 70 cells to speed up computation.

Finally, note that the mixed discrete-continuous investment framework allows for different specifications of the capital stock adjustment cost function $c(i, k)$. In the empirical application of Chapter 4, capital stock adjustment costs are a (quadratic) function of gross investment. As noted earlier, this is standard practice in empirical applications (because measurement problems are usually assumed to be more severe for the capital stock than for investment, see Hamermesh and Pfann (1996)). An alternative would be to model adjustment costs as a function of the existing capital stock. This implies that capital stock adjustment costs are linked directly to the corresponding state variable. Such an approach would be interesting as it reflects the notion of lumpy (i. e., fixed) capital adjustment costs (scaled by plant size as measured by capital stock), but has not yet been used in empirical work.

3.3.2 A note on time-varying discount rates

In the general formulation of Markov decision processes (MDPs, see Table 3.1), the discount factor is allowed to vary over time as well as to depend on the agent's current states and decisions. When deriving solutions to Markov decision problems, the assumption is made that the discount factor β is constant over time and independent of states and controls. This is actually one of the central properties of stationary MDPs. While existence and uniqueness of the solution to the underlying intertemporal optimization problem can be established without this assumption (a discount rate that is uniformly bounded away from unity suffices to ensure the crucial contraction property), no stationary policy could be derived, and this in turn would destroy the econometric estimation approach for DDP models discussed in Section 3.2.3. This is the reason why in this study, the assumption of a constant discount rate β is maintained throughout.

In models of individual behavior, a fixed discount rate can be justified because it reflects the agent's rate of time preference which in turn can be assumed to be a "deep" preference parameter that does neither vary over time nor depend on states and controls. In the case of firms' decisions, the discount factor reflects, *inter alia*, the interest rate at which the firm can obtain outside funds. These interest rates can vary over time (over the business cycle), and it is also conceivable that the interest rate depends on the quality of investment projects undertaken by the firm, as judged by lenders (under asymmetric information). While there are many structural empirical studies that treat the discount rate as either entirely fixed or at least not state-dependent (often without even discussing the implications), there are theoretical reasons to be concerned with such an approach (see, e. g., Blanchard and Fischer (1989), p. 294, for a discussion).

In this study, the assumption is made that there exists a constant discount factor β, while all other variations in the interest rate and the risk premium are treated as latent variables: Although this structure acknowledges that the risk premium is state-dependent in general, no effort is made to model this dependence explicitly. To illustrate the effects of a fixed discount factor β, think of the "true" discount rate $\tilde{\beta}_t(s_t, a_t)$ as being the product of a component that reflects a risk-free interest rate, r, and a time and state-dependent risk premium, $\rho_t(s_t, a_t)$:

$$\tilde{\beta}_t(s_t, a_t) = \frac{1}{1+r} \cdot \rho_t(s_t, a_t) = \beta \cdot \rho_t(s_t, a_t)\,. \tag{3.36}$$

In the Markov decision problem, $\rho_t(s_t, a_t)$ is absorbed in the value function, hence this formulation ensures the existence of a fixed discount rate β. Note that the risk-free interest rate that is hidden in β can be made arbitrarily small, as long as it is positive. Also, when estimating a DDP model on individual or firm data, researchers have usually had difficulties with the precise estimation of β, and hence β is usually fixed at some arbitrary value (Rust and Phelan (1997) use $\beta = .98$, for example). The same approach is used in this study: In the estimation exercise presented in Section 4.6, the discount rate is fixed at .99, corresponding to an annual risk-free rate of 1.01 %. This assumption seems to be defendable.

Second, consider how the risk premium $\rho_t(s, a)$ can be treated in the formulation and estimation of a DDP model of firm behavior. In principle, it is possible to model the dependence of the risk premium on states and control explicitly, but in practice this will be quite hard: While models of credit rationing such as Stiglitz and Weiss (1981) rely on the notion that the interest rate offered to firms depends on the (to the lender, unobservable) quality of a project, there seems to be no simple closed-form relationship that maps observable state variables into a risk premium.

If one chooses not to model explicitly the time and state dependence of the risk premium (as I do), stochastic variations in the scale of the profit function must be interpreted as reflecting variations in the risk premium. In the econometric estimation, these variations are eventually absorbed by the error structure of the nested fixed-point algorithm, i. e., by the unobservable state variables. This interpretation is satisfactory regarding time-varying interest rates because they are a macroeconomic shock in the sense of Assumption CI-M; hence time-varying interest rates do not affect the asymptotic properties of the NFXP estimator.

The conditional independence assumption will be violated, however, if the interest rate faced by the firm depends on the plant-level state variables. Therefore, estimating a plant-level investment model with the NFXP estimator amounts to assuming that either the interest rate faced by the firm is not state-dependent at all, or at least not dependent on the states of individual plants. The latter version might have some appeal, but I do not wish to push this argument too far. Note also that this implicit independence assumption can be tested (jointly with any other structural assumption) when the model is subjected to an omnibus specification test.

Overall, treating interest rates as latent variables in the empirical model of firm investment and as nuisance parameters in estimation is unsatisfactory from a theoretical view but difficult to avoid given the econometric framework for structual estimation of DDPs and the absence of clear theoretical advise how plant-level state variables affect the interest rate faced by the firm. Note also that standard structural models of firm investment such as the Euler equation models considered by Whited (1994) and Oliner *et al.* (1995) allow only for time-varying interest rates as well, ignoring any state dependence.

3.A Appendix: mathematical results

For quick reference, this appendix collects formal statements of some definitions and results. Results are stated only if they have a direct economic interpretation that relates to the chapter's substantive issues, however. General references for this material are Rust (1996), and the monographs by Naylor and Sell (1982) and Stokey and Lucas (1989), the former being slightly more formal, and the latter offering many economic applications.

Definition: Contraction mapping

Let (X, ρ) be a metric space and $f : X \to X$. We say that f is a contraction mapping if there is a real number $\beta \in [0, 1)$ such that $\rho(f(x), f(y)) \leq \beta \rho(x, y)$ for all $x, y \in X$.

Remarks: It follows from the definition that a contraction mapping is uniformly continuous. The constant β is called the *Lipschitz coefficient* or *modulus* of f.

Theorem: Contraction mapping theorem

Let (X, ρ) be a complete metric space and let $f : X \to X$ be a contraction. Then there exists one and only one point $x_0 \in X$ such that

$$f(x_0) = x_0 \,.$$

Moreover, if x is any point in X and x_n is defined inductively by $x_1 = f(x), x_2 = f(x_1), \ldots, x_n = f(x_{n-1})$, then $x_n \to x_0$ as $n \to \infty$.

Proof: See Naylor and Sell (1982), pp. 126–127, or Stokey and Lucas (1989), pp. 50–52.

Remarks: The contraction mapping theorem states that f has a unique fixed point x_0 and that every sequence of iterations of f converges to this fixed point. This property is used extensively in the numerical solution of functional equations, as discussed in Section 3.1.

Theorem: Blackwell's sufficient conditions for a contraction

Let $X \subseteq I\!R$, and let $B(X)$ be a space of bounded functions $f : X \to I\!R$, with the supremum norm. Let $T : B(X) \to B(X)$ be an operator satisfying the following conditions:

1. *Monotonicity:* For all $x \in X$ and $f, g \in B(X)$, $f(x) \leq g(x)$ implies $T(f)(x) \leq T(g)(x)$.

2. *Discounting:* There exists some $\beta \in [0, 1)$ such that for all $f \in B(X)$, $a \geq 0$, $x \in X$, $T[(f + a)](x) \leq T(f)(x) + \beta a$.

Then T is a contraction with modulus β.

Proof: See Stokey and Lucas (1989), p. 54.

Theorem: Lebesgue dominated convergence theorem

Let $(S, \mathcal{S}, \mu)$ be a measure space, and let $\{f_n\}$ be a sequence of integrable functions that converges almost everywhere to a measurable function f. If there exists an integrable function g such that $|f_n| \leq g$ for all n, then f is integrable and $\int f \, \mathrm{d}\mu = \lim_{n \to \infty} \int f_n \, \mathrm{d}\mu$.

Proof: See Naylor and Sell (1982), p. 579, or Stokey and Lucas (1989), pp. 192–193.

Remarks: If the functions $\{f_n\}$ are uniformely bounded, and if μ is a finite measure (both of which hold in the applications considered in this study), the Lebesgue dominated convergence theorem applies trivially as the function g can be taken to be constant and equal to the uniform bound on the sequence $\{f_n\}$.

Theorem: Blackwell's (1965) theorem

Given an infinite-horizon, stationary Markov decision process satisfying the regularity conditions in Bhattacharya and Majumdar (1989), it holds that:

1. A unique solution V to Bellman's equation (3.6) exists, and it coincides with the agent's expected discounted utility under an optimal policy.

2. An optimal decision rule $\alpha = (\alpha(s), \alpha(s), \ldots)$ exists and coincides with the stationary, non-random, Markovian optimal control given by the solution to (3.2).

Proof: See Bhattacharya and Majumdar (1989) or Rust (1994c), p. 17–18. Note that the proof relies on the observation that $\lim_{T \to \infty} V_T(s) = V_\infty(s)$ for all $s \in S$, which in turn follows from the Lebesgue dominated convergence theorem just stated. This shows also that in applications, boundedness of the value function must be insured.

Remarks: The most important regularity conditions (for economic applications) are covered by Assumption MDP. An important issue concerns the boundedness of the state and decision spaces and the utility function. The regularity conditions established by Bhattacharya and Majumdar (1989) are somewhat weaker than those in Blackwell (1965): They cover also the semi-Markov case and allow for unbounded, upper semi-continuous (in s and a) utility functions $u(s, a)$. Note, however, that the computational methods described in this chapter require bounded state and decision spaces, so we maintain this assumption throughout (see Rust (1996), p. 636). Boundedness is necessary to ensure the contraction property which is required by the numerical algorithm, while existence and uniqueness themselves do not require the contraction property (see Bhattacharya and Majumdar (1989), p. 375).

Theorem: Differentiability of the value function (Benveniste and Scheinkman (1979))

Let $X \subseteq I\!R^L$ be a convex set, let $F : X \to I\!R$ be concave, let $x_0 \in \text{int}\, X$, and let $\tilde{X}$ be a neighborhood of x_0. If there is a concave, differentiable function $\tilde{F} : \tilde{X} \to I\!R$, with $\tilde{F}(x_0) = F(x_0)$ and with $\tilde{F}(x) \leq F(x)$ for all $x \in \tilde{X}$, then F is differentiable at x_0, and the partial derivatives at x_0 are given by $F_i(x_0) = \tilde{F}_i(x_o), i = 1, \ldots, L$.

Proof: See, e. g., Stokey and Lucas (1989), p. 84.

Theorem: Optimal decisions in Euler class CDPs (Rust (1994c))

Let $\alpha(y, z)$ be the optimal decision rule and V be the value function for an Euler class CDP characterized by the Bellman equation (3.8). If $y \in \text{int}\, Y$ and $\alpha \in \text{int}\, A(y, z)$, and if $V(y, z)$ is a continuously differentiable function of y at the point (y, z), then its derivative is given by:

$$\frac{\partial V(y, z)}{\partial y} = \frac{\partial u(y, z, \alpha(y, z)}{\partial y} - \frac{\partial u(y, z, \alpha(y, z)}{\partial a} h(y, z, \alpha(y, z)) \,. \quad (3.37)$$

Proof: See Stokey and Lucas (1989), pp. 266–267, and Rust (1994c). Note that the proof relies primarily on the differentiability theorem for CDPs established by Benveniste and Scheinkman (1979).

Remarks: If the decision problem satisfies the conditions listed in Table 3.2, including concavity of $V(\cdot)$, then for any y and z, the optimal choice $\alpha(y, z)$ is unique.

Chapter 4

Plant-level investment and exit decisions and firm-level financial status

In this chapter, I review alternative measures of financial constraints at the firm level and discuss how such firm-level measures can be linked with plant-level data in the empirical analysis of firm investment under financial constraints. The empirical study presented in this chapter has three purposes. First, it shows how plant-level and firm-level data can (and as I will argue, should) be combined to develop a better understanding of how a firm's financial situation influences both its investment and exit (i.e., plant closure or sell-off) decisions. Second, I use a new measure of a firm's financial status, designed to alleviate some well-known drawbacks of static sample-split approaches used in much of the earlier literature. Third, the econometric analysis uses both reduced-form and structural approaches, and I illustrate how the results of the structural estimation exercise can be used in policy simulations.

The identification of financially constrained firms is not an easy task. Approaches that rely on some form of static sample-split criterion cannot fully characterize a firm's financial status. Therefore, I use an alternative approach which is based on an ordinal, time-varying financial status indicator proposed by Kaplan and Zingales (1997). This new measure has only recently been developed, and it has some problems of its own (primarily due to the small number of firms for which this measure currently exists). The evidence I present here, however, indicates that the effort involved in constructing such measures results in better information on firms' financial status.

After a brief overview of the empirical approach in Section 4.1, Section 4.2 contains a detailed discussion of the financial status variable. The empirical model of plant-level investment and exit decisions under financial constraints is presented in Section 4.3, and the construction of the dataset is discussed in Section 4.4. Next, I present two econometric models based on the dynamic discrete-choice model of investment and exit decisions of Section 3.3. The first model is a reduced-form two-equation model of plant growth (Section 4.5). Then, I present results for a structural model of investment and exit decisons and perform a policy simulation exercise based on these estimates (Section 4.6). The empirical findings are summarized in Section 4.7. A detailed discussion of the data sources and the construction of the variables used in this paper can be found in the data appendix.

4.1 Introduction and overview

The objective of the empirical study presented in this chapter is to assess whether financial constraints influence firms' investment and exit decisions. For the purpose of this chapter, a firm is defined to be financially constrained if "the cost or availability of external funds precludes the company from making an investment it would have chosen to make had internal funds been available" (Kaplan and Zingales (1997)). One possible reason for financial constraints is credit rationing, i. e., a situation in which borrowers cannot borrow as much as they would like, given an unconstrained optimization model with complete financial markets. There are various reasons why credit rationing might occur in equilibrium; such models are mainly based on incomplete or asymmetric information between borrowers and lenders (here, firms and banks), resulting in incomplete or imperfect financial markets.

The effects of financial constraints on firm behavior have received much attention in recent years; the related literature is the subject of Section 2.2. From that review, recall that there are essentially three different levels of aggregation at which these effects have been investigated. At the micro (firm) level, the availability of outside finance has been identified as a major determinant of firm growth and survival. Because of financial constraints, firms may be prevented from realizing promising projects they have at hand, or even from undertaking R&D in the first place. Once a firm has started an investment project or entered a market with a new product, it may still be driven out because of a lack of funds. Both effects of incomplete capital markets are obviously not desirable from a welfare view. This leads to the industry level, where both industrial and financial economists have studied the role of capital markets in industrial restructuring; these models also rely on a link between the firm's financial status and its investment policies. Welfare implications of financial constraints can be different here: Financial constraints (i. e., the fact that pressure is put on firms' management by outside suppliers of funds) can prevent overinvestment in general, and can help to reduce excess capacity in declining industries by forcing firms to exit. These effects of financial constraints involve efficiency gains and might increase aggregate welfare (although the latter issue is subject to an ongoing debate). Finally, there is a macroeconomic literature which interprets the sensitivity of firm investment to financial constraints as a central part of the credit (or lending) channel of monetary policy transmission. These models argue that imperfections in capital markets, resulting for example in credit constraints, can lead to or exacerbate business cycle fluctuations by propagating relatively modest monetary (and in some models, also real) shocks.

I have also noted that while there are quite a few theoretical models of the influence of financial constraints on firm investment (with important policy implications at the firm, industry, and macro levels), empirical evidence is still mixed. Finding evidence of a relationship between financial constraints and investment decisions would not only support the view that there is a credit channel of monetary policy, but might also help to design and evaluate government programs that support small, growing firms which are thought to be most affected by financial constraints, given their limited access to capital markets.

There are several empirical studies which confirm the sensitivity of firm investment to financial constraints. A prominent example is the paper by Fazzari *et al.* (1988); they were the first to report empirical evidence on the existence of credit rationing using firm panel data. Their empirical approach has since been refined along various dimensions. (Again, see Section 2.2 for details.) This project attempts to address three remaining objections that have been raised against earlier empirical tests:

- Using firm-level data might introduce aggregation biases into empirical models of investment decisions. The dynamics of investment spending at the plant level seem to be much richer than firm-level data would suggest. It is therefore likely that the effects of financial constraints are most severe at the plant level and at least partially washed out when investment is aggregated to the firm level.

- Most studies of financial constraints and investment decisions have used balanced panels of continuing firms, hence ignoring selection biases due to endogenous market exits (which might well be related to the firm's financial status). Market exits are also more likely to occur at the plant level first: Before whole firms are closed, it is likely that some of its plants are closed or sold.
- The standard approach to identifying financially constrained firms uses indicators such as firm size or some balance-sheet variable (e. g., the dividend payout ratio or leverage) as a sample-split criterion. This approach has been challenged by Kaplan and Zingales (1997); their arguments are reviewed in Section 4.2 below. They propose an alternative measure of a firm's financial status. Its main advantages are, first, that it takes into account non-balance sheet information, and second, that it is allowed to vary over time, reflecting changes in macroeconomic conditions and/or the firm's financial policy.

The empirical approach to analyzing firm behavior under financial constraints suggested in this study tries to address these issues in a consistent framework, the dynamic programming model of firms' investment and market exit decisions derived in Section 3.3.[49] This model, which is of independent interest in the investment and firm dynamics literature, is extended here to allow using information on firm-level financial constraints. In particular, I use the concept of a firm's financial status and the ordinary indicator variable introduced by Kaplan and Zingales (1997). Because this indicator variable is allowed to vary over time, this approach can also address business cycle aspects much better than static sample-split approaches. This research strategy follows Kaplan and Zingales by focusing on the effects of capital market imperfections on investment (rather than trying to identify the sources of the capital market imperfections at work).

[49] Of course, neither aspect is new to empirical studies of firm behavior. However, to the best of my knowledge they have not yet been jointly considered in empirical studies of financial constraints.

The central simplifying assumption needed to make the model operational is that the firm's financial decisions are separated from the structural model of plant-level investment and exit decisions. This approach does not amount to a full structural model of firm behavior, but it allows for a consistent treatment of investment and exit decisions at the plant level, taking firm-level financial status as given.[50]

The sample used in this study is essentially that considered by Kaplan and Zingales (1997) which is, in turn, based on the group of firms identified as being financially constrained by Fazzari *et al.* (1988). The dataset itself consists primarily of plant-level data on output and factor inputs, including investment spending, for all plants owned by these firms during the 1972–84 period. These plant-level observations, taken from the Longitudinal Research Database, are matched with data on the respective firm's financial status. Firm-level data are, first, the ordinal financial status indicator constructed by Kaplan and Zingales, and second, for comparison with standard approaches, balance-sheet variables from Compustat.

For econometric estimation, I use two quite different approaches: a long-established reduced-form model of plant growth which allows to control for observed plant exits, and a modified version of the dynamic programming model of joint plant-level investment and exit decisions presented in Section 3.3. Estimation of the structural model is based on Rust's (1987, 1988) nested fixed-point algorithm (see Section 3.2.3). The estimation results obtained from the structural model are finally used for a policy simulation exercise.

4.2 Alternative measures of a firm's financial status

A broad characterization of financially constrained firms is that their costs of external funds are higher than their costs of internal funds (i. e., cash flow). Starting with the seminal paper by Fazzari *et al.* (1988),

---

[50] A natural extension would be to make firm-level financial variables endogenous, say, by including financial assets as a state variable in the optimization model, as suggested by Pakes (1994) and discussed in Section 3.3. However, neither would such a model be amenable to structural estimation given current techniques, nor do databases exist with sufficient information *both* on production and investment decisions and on financial variables.

many empirical tests of the sensitivity of investment to the availability of internal funds use sample-split approaches to identify financially constrained firms. The criterion used by Fazzari *et al.* (1988) is the firm's dividend-income ratio. The rationale is that "if the cost disadvantage of external funds is large, it should have the greatest effect on firms that retain most of their income. If the cost disadvantage is slight, then retention practices should reveal little about financing practices, q values, or investment behavior." (p. 158) Using the dividend-income ratio criterion, they divide their sample of 422 firms continuously contained in the Valueline database over the 1970–84 period into three subsamples. The classification scheme is reproduced in Table 4.1.

Table 4.1: The sample-split criterion used by Fazzari *et al.* (1988)

Category	Dividend-income ratio	Firms	
1	Less than 10 %[a]	49	11.6 %
2	Between 10 % and 20 %[a]	39	9.2 %
3	20 % and above	334	79.1 %
Total		422	

Source: Fazzari *et al.* (1988), Table 2.
[a] For at least 10 years.

Kaplan and Zingales (1997) criticize both the theoretical foundation of the test strategy proposed by Fazzari *et al.* (1988) and the empirical implementation of the sample-split criterion. They argue that the fundamental assumption of this literature, namely that the investment-cash flow sensitivity (tested by either reduced-form or structural methods) increases monotonically with the degree of financing constraints, is theoretically ill-posed. While it is clear that a financially constrained firm's investment should be sensitive to internal cash flow and an unconstrained firm's investment should not, it is not clear that the degree of this sensitivity should vary with the degree of financial constraints. Given that investment of the vast majority of firms analyzed by Fazzari *et al.* (1988) is sensitive to cash flow, this monotonicity assumption is crucial for standard sample-split approaches to be valid.

The central idea of Kaplan and Zingales's (1997) approach is to construct an ordinal measure for the financial status of firms that conveys more information than the sample-split approach. Their scheme "is designed to distinguish relative differences in the degree to which firms are financially constrained" (p. 173). They use a variety of sources "to derive as complete a picture as possible of the availability if internal and external funds for each firm as well as each firm's demand for funds" (p. 170). In addition to standard balance-sheet information such as leverage and cash flow, they use complementary sources of information. These are management's letters to the shareholders, the discussion of liquidity and financial status in annual reports, the 10-K reports that most publicly traded corporations in the U.S. have to file annually with the SEC, and other sources such as publicly available news pieces (taken from the Wall Street Journal Index). In the 10-K reports, for example, firms are explicitly required to discuss their liquidity, capital resources, and results of operations.

Table 4.2: The financial status indicator by Kaplan and Zingales (1997)

Category	Financial status (annual)	Firm years[a]	
0	Not financially constrained	389	53.4 %
1	Likely not financially constrained	233	32.0 %
2	Possibly financially constrained	53	7.3 %
3	Likely financially constrained	34	4.7 %
4	Financially constrained	20	2.7 %
Total		729	

Source: Kaplan and Zingales (1997), Appendix.

[a] Six firm years (1970–73 for Commodore Intl. Ltd. and 1970–71 for James River Corp.) are missing in the Kaplan-Zingales sample, so the total number of firm-year observations is $49 \times 15 - 6 = 729$.

Kaplan and Zingales use this information to construct an ordinal indicator that groups each firm-year observation into one of five categories (the exact definitions are listed in Table 4.2). The 49 firms considered by Kaplan and Zingales are those classified as financially constrained by Fazzari *et al.* (1988) because of their low dividend-income ratios, i. e., the 49 Class 1 firms in Table 4.1; Table 4.3 contains a list of these firms.

The most important result of this new classification scheme is that surprisingly few firms are financially constrained, both on an annual basis and over the entire sample period. Table 4.2 shows that less than 15 % of all firm-year observations are classified as possibly, likely, or definitely financially constrained. Based on this annual financial status indicator, Kaplan and Zingales also assign the 49 firms to three groups according to their overall financial situation over the entire 1970–84 period; this grouping is reflected in Table 4.3. Kaplan and Zingales find 19 firms to be not or likely not financially constrained over the entire sample period, while only 22 firms (less than half of the sample) have some years during which they were likely financially constrained or definitely financially constrained.

Figure 4.1 shows the annual financial status variable for three representative firms, one from each of the three groups identified by Kaplan and Zingales, over the entire sample period, 1970–84. The Group 1 firm, Cameron Iron Works, was always classified as not financially constrained; Coherent, the Group 2 firm, has a string of years with a likely not financially constrained status and three possibly financially constrained years, while the Group 3 firm, Katy Industries, has a six-year episode (1974–79) during which it was rated definitely financially constrained, likely financially constrained, or possibly financially constrained.

These examples illustrate one of the major conceptual strengths of Kaplan and Zingales's classification scheme: The financial status variable varies over time, and the financial status histories of the 49 firms in the sample are quite heterogenous. For example, even most Group 3 firms have spells during which they were *not* classified as being financially constrained or likely financially constrained. These observations highlight the fact that a time-varying measure such as the financial status indicator by Kaplan and Zingales conveys much more detailed information about firms' financial situation than standard sample-split approaches.

The main finding reported by Kaplan and Zingales is that those firms they classify as *less* financially constrained show *higher* sensitivities of investment to cash flow. In Kaplan and Zingales's view, this result contradicts the results of existing empirical studies which argue that investment is sensitive to internal finance when a firm is financially constrained.

The financial status variable constructed by Kaplan and Zingales can be criticized for a number of reasons; see the response by Fazzari *et al.*

Table 4.3: The 49 firms analyzed by Kaplan and Zingales (1997)

Group 1	Group 2	Group 3
Barry (R.G.)	Coachmen Industries Inc.	Adams Russell
Cameron Iron Works	Coherent Inc.	Analog Devices
Data General Corp.	Commodore Intl. Ltd.	Applied Magnetics Corp.
DWG Corp.	Nucor Corp.	Aydin Corp.
Digital Equipment	Plantronics	Champion Home Builders
Fluke (John) Mfg. Co.	Teradyne Inc.	Coleco
Forest Laboratories	Vernitron	Compugraphic
GCA Corp.	Whitehall Cement Mfg. Co.	Control Data Corp.
Helene Curtis Industries		Cordis Corp.
Hewlett Packard Co.		Galveston Houston
Iroquois Brands Ltd.		Gerber Scientific Inc.
James River Corp.		Hesston
National Semiconductor		Intl. Rectifier Corp.
Scientific Atlanta Inc.		Katy Industries
Southdown Inc.		Mohawk Data Sciences
Thermo Electron Corp.		Raychem Corp.
Trico Industries		Recognition Equipment Inc.
Wang Laboratories		Rockcor Inc.
Winnebago Industries		Rogers Corp.
		SCI Systems Inc.
		Tyson Foods Inc.
		U.S. Surgical Corp.

Source: Kaplan and Zingales (1997), Appendix.
Notes: The 49 firms in the Kaplan-Zingales sample are those classified as financially constrained by Fazzari *et al.* (1988). Here, these firms are grouped according to Kaplan and Zingales's financial status classification for the entire sample period, 1970–84, defined as follows:-
Group 1: not financially constrained or likely not financially constrained in every year;
Group 2: possibly financially constrained in some year;
Group 3: likely financially constrained or financially constrained in some year.

(1996).[51] First of all, the classification scheme is highly judgemental, and as no specific guidelines for the classification were reported by Kaplan and Zingales, their approach is difficult to replicate for other samples of firms. Arguably, the most important question that arises is whether in

[51] The response by Fazzari *et al.* (1996) was based on an earlier version of the paper, Kaplan and Zingales (1995). In the published version, Kaplan and Zingales (1997) already address some of the concerns brought forth by Fazzari *et al.*

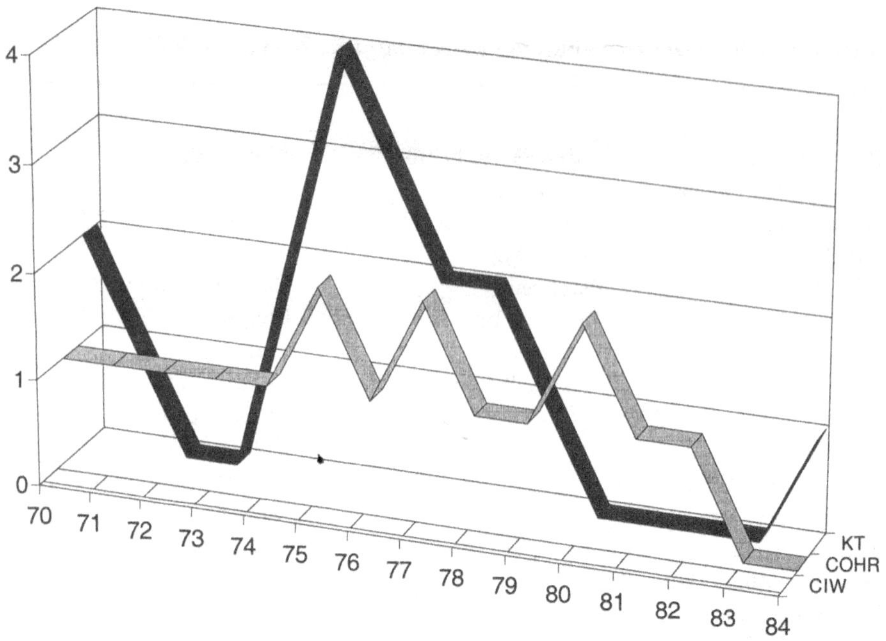

Figure 4.1: Firm-level financial status for three selected firms, 1970–84

Source: Kaplan and Zingales (1997), Appendix.

Notes: CIW: Cameron Iron Works; COHR: Coherent Inc.; KT: Katy Industries. – These firms were chosen from the full sample of 49 firms; they are not necessarily in the sample of 40 firms that were matched with LRD plant-level data.

the data sources used by Kaplan and Zingales, managers report truthfully on their financial status. For a variety of reasons, Kaplan and Zingales do not consider misreporting a serious problem for their research design, see their paper (p. 182) for details. Also, Fazzari *et al.* argue that the criterion emphasizes financial distress rather than financing constraints. A more general objection by Fazzari *et al.* is that, given the problems they see with the definition of the financial constraints indicator, Kaplan and Zingales make unrealistically fine distinctions in the firm's availability of finance. Fazzari *et al.* also raise some doubts about the econometric results obtained by Kaplan and Zingales using their new indicator. (However, this objection is not related to the indicator itself, but rather to econometric problems.)

Despite these objections, it seems worthwhile to further investigate the new indicator variable constructed by Kaplan and Zingales. In particular, it will be interesting to see whether variations in this variable over the sample period help to explain firms' investment decisions. Such a finding would confirm that the new variable contains useful information about firms' financial status and that financial status – as defined and measured by Kaplan and Zingales – does indeed affect investment.

4.3 The empirical model of firm behavior under financial constraints

In this section, I discuss the empirical approach taken in this study in order to investigate the influence of firm-level financial constraints on plant-level investment and exit decisions. The central idea is to combine firm-level financial data and plant-level production/investment data to test whether the financial situation of a firm influences its investment decisions (as observed at the plant level). Using these different levels of aggregation requires an empirical model of finance and investment decisions within an existing firm. This model is illustrated in Figure 4.2.

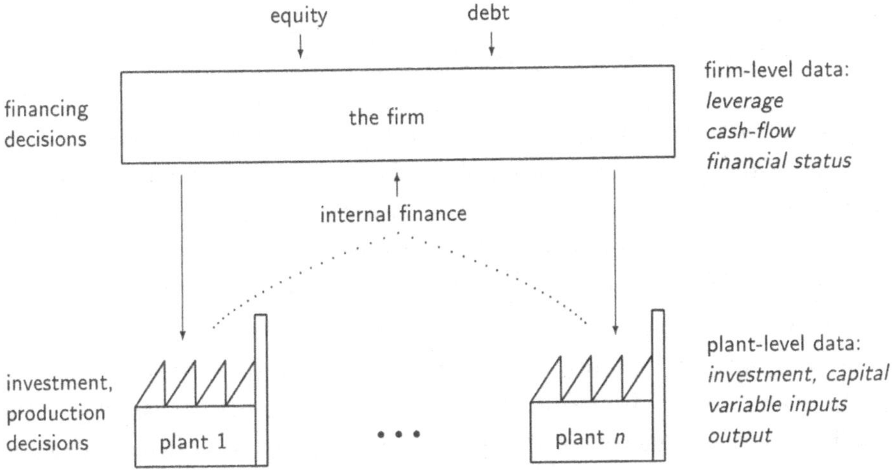

Figure 4.2: Firm-level finance and plant-level decisions in the empirical model

At the firm level, the firm chooses its financing policies, resulting in its current capital structure. Outside borrowing might be subject to credit constraints, and for some firms (presumably the smaller ones), raising equity might be difficult as well. Either problem would result in financial constraints at the firm level. In addition to these outside sources of finance, the firm can also use its cash flow to finance investment. This model takes the firm's financial decisions and any outside restrictions as given; hence the firm's capital structure is exogenous to the model. As discussed in Section 2.2, this is a standard approach in the theoretical and empirical literature on intertemporal investment decisions under financial constraints. While such an assumption is not entirely satisfying theoretically, it is difficult to explicitly include a firm's financing decisions under asymmetric information in a dynamic model of investment decisions (see, e. g., Milne and Robertson (1996)).

The model further assumes that aggregated (firm-level) cash flow is exogenous at the plant level. This assumption is clearly restrictive; its implications are discussed below. Under these assumptions, the firm's financial decisions can be treated as a black box in the empirical model, and its financial situation can be described by variables observed at the firm level. In this study, these variables are leverage (the ratio of long-term debt to total assets), cash flow, and the financial status indicator developed by Kaplan and Zingales (1997).

Given its financial status, the firm makes its investment decisions, i. e., it allocates funds to the individual plants for capital investment. If the firm is not financially constrained, these investment decisions will be the solutions to individual intertemporal optimization problems for each plant, just as in the theoretical model derived in Section 3.3. (The model also allows to choose zero investment or to close or sell the plant entirely.) The capital stock installed at each plant is then a quasi-fixed factor, and output and factor input decisions are made at the plant level, given the capital stock and factor prices. This model of plant-level investment and production decisions uses only variables observed at the plant level: investment (and the resulting capital stock), variable inputs, and output. If, however, the firm is financially constrained, firm-level financial variables should be significant in the plant-level regressions, i. e., financial constraints affect plant-level investment after controlling for other determinants such as productivity and expected market demand. This is the central empirical idea used in this study.

In general, plant-level investment/production decisions also determine the plant-level cash flows, which can be aggregated to firm-level cash flow. Firm-level cash flow, in turn, is a major component of the firm's financial situation, and it enters the plant-level regressions both directly and through its effect on the firm-level financial status variable. Hence, firm-level financial variables should properly be treated as endogenous in the plant-level model of investment and exit decisions. There are two major difficulties with this (and thus the current specification of the model treats firm-level financial status as exogenous at the plant level). First, taking account of this endogeneity in the structual econometric model would require to implement some plant-level expectation mechanism for the next period's firm-level financial situation, which in turn would depend on *all* the cash flows of all plants. Current theories of firms' internal finance do not offer any clear-cut advice how this interdependence should enter a structual model (see, e. g., Gertner *et al.* (1994) and Stein (1997) and the discussion in Section 2.2). In any case, plant-level investment decisions could not be treated individually, and the resulting modifications would make it difficult to estimate the model. Implicitly, the model used here assumes that the allocation of funds is sticky across plants, i. e., if the firm moves into a financially constrained state, this restriction is transmitted uniformly to all plants.[52]

The second problem is related to the data sources used in this study. As will become clear in the next section, data are available only for all *manufacturing* plants that belong to a given firm. It is, however, likely that large firms generate cash flow from non-manufacturing sources as well. The importance of these sources would be difficult to assess in practice, but it could effectively wash out an individual plant's effect on firm-level financial status.[53] Both problems together imply that the exogeneity assumption for firm-level financial status is difficult to relax if investment and production data are at the plant level. The advantages of

---

52 This assumption is consistent with the empirical findings of Shin and Stulz (1996), but inconsistent with some other theoretical and empirical studies in the recent literature on internal capital markets; see Section 2.2.

53 Lamont (1997), for example, presents a case study that illustrates how shocks to firm-level financial status affect investment across very different operations of a large corporation.

plant-level data in the analysis of investment decisions might, however, outweigh the damage done by imposing such assumptions.

To sum up, the maintained hypothesis of the empirical approach used in this chapter is that decisions within a firm can be split into a number of distinct components: Current production and variable factor demand decisions are made at the plant level; they are perfectly observable given plant-level data. Investment and market entry/exit decisions are made at the firm level, subject to financial status, for each individual plant. For each period, investment and entry/exit decisions are interpreted as assigning a rate of investment to each plant (or, selling or closing it). Hence, this study uses a two-step empirical strategy:

- Investment and market exit decisions are investigated using both a reduced-form and a structural approach based on the solution to the firm's intertemporal optimization problem reflected in the mixed discrete-continuous investment model of Section 3.3.1.

  Estimation of the investment model is performed using plant-level data.

- These models are supplemented with indicator variables for the firm's financial situation; this allows to assess the effects of firm-level financial constraints for plant-level investment.

4.4 Description of the plant-level dataset

The main data source used in this study is the Longitudinal Research Database (LRD). All plant-level nominal investment, variable factor demand and output data as well as the information on plant operating status were obtained from the LRD. This section concentrates on the selection of firms and plants for the estimation dataset and presents some descriptive statistics. Further details on the construction of the dataset can be found in the data appendix. The LRD is discussed in Section 4.A.1. For the process of actually retrieving these data from the LRD and building an unbalanced panel, see Section 4.A.2, and for the construction of the variables used for estimation, see Section 4.A.3.

The 49 firms contained in Kaplan and Zingales's sample were matched with LRD plants using a name matching procedure. In total, data on

Table 4.4: Details of the data cleaning process

	Observations
Raw sample	3989
Single observation spells	169
First observation of each remaining spell	573
Plant-years with zero output or input	160
Plant-years lost due to outlier trimming	73
Cleaned sample (final panel)	3014

Source: Longitudinal Research Database (LRD), U.S. Bureau of the Census; and own calculations.

plants owned by 40 of these 49 firms were matched with LRD plant-level data.[54] The raw sample with 3989 plant-year observations was then cleaned. First, spells with just one observation were dropped; then, the first year of each remaining spell was excluded. (This is due to the fact that the first year of each spell is used to construct state variables for the following year.) Finally, plant-year observations with zero output or input were dropped, and the sample was trimmed for outliers.[55] Table 4.4 contains details of the data cleaning process. The resulting panel has 444 plants with 573 distinct spells and a total of 3014 plant-year observations (see Table 4.5). Note that a surprisingly large fraction (almost 30%) of these plant spells ends with a plant exit (exit is defined as the plant being either closed or sold to another firm).

Table 4.6 reports the distribution of plant spells. Note that the observed spells are actually one year longer as the first plant-year observation of each spell is used to construct the second year's state variables. As one can see, there is a fairly large number of plant spells which cover the whole 12-year period (1973–84); but there are also many very short spells. Many of these short spells occur in the first years of the dataset;

[54] For confidentiality reasons, the names of these 40 firms cannot be disclosed; neither can a number of otherwise desireable descriptive statistics on the matched sub-sample of firms be reported.

[55] An observation was excluded if any of the following ratios was above the 99.5 percentile of the respective ratio's sample distribution: output/labor, output/materials, output/capital, capital/labor, investment/capital. Outliers in these ratios typically indicate errors in one of the variables involved.

Table 4.5: Sample characteristics

	Raw sample		Cleaned sample[a]	
Firms	40		40	
Plants	514		444	
Operating status: sold	176	34.2%	100	22.5%
Operating status: closed	86	16.7%	30	6.8%
Total exits	262	59.0%	130	29.3%
Plant spells	742		573	
Plant-year observations	3989		3014	

Source: Longitudinal Research Database (LRD), U.S. Bureau of the Census; and own calculations.

[a] The cleaned sample is the sample used for estimation.

Table 4.6: Distribution of plant spell lengths

Years	Plants	
1	92	16.1 %
2	83	14.5 %
3	61	10.7 %
4	56	9.8 %
5	35	6.1 %
6	68	11.9 %
7	27	4.7 %
8	25	4.4 %
9	19	3.3 %
10	30	5.2 %
11	18	3.1 %
12	59	10.3 %
Total	573	

Source: Longitudinal Research Database (LRD), U.S. Bureau of the Census; and own calculations.

these spells are potentially much longer, but the full plant history cannot be observed due to left-truncation. In the model used in this study, left-truncation is not a serious problem due to its Markovian structure: All historic information is contained in the current period's state variables (which are actually lagged values). The only critical variable, then, is plant age, but as discussed in Section 4.A.2, one can use some information on plant age from the LRD which goes back to the years before 1972 (the first year in which the other variables are observed).

Table 4.7: Industry distribution of plant-year observations (cleaned sample)

SIC	Industry	Plant years	
20	Food and kindred products	336	11.2 %
23	Apparel and other textile products	16	0.5 %
24	Lumber and wood products	60	2.0 %
25	Furniture and fixtures	16	0.5 %
26	Paper and allied products	423	14.0 %
27	Printing and publishing	20	0.7 %
28	Chemicals and allied products	83	2.8 %
30	Rubber and misc. plastics products	35	1.2 %
31	Leather and leather products	81	2.7 %
32	Stone, clay, and glass products	48	1.6 %
33	Primary metal industries	81	2.7 %
34	Fabricated metal products	137	4.6 %
35	Industrial machinery and equipment	634	21.0 %
36	Electronic and other electric equipment	453	15.0 %
37	Transportation equipment	141	4.7 %
38	Instruments and related products	380	12.6 %
39	Misc. manufacturing industries	70	2.3 %
Total		3014	

Source: Longitudinal Research Database (LRD), U.S. Bureau of the Census; and own calculations.

Table 4.7 contains details on the 2-digit industry decomposition of the sample; almost the entire manufacturing sector is covered with at least some plant-year observations in most 2-digit industries. (The LRD also contains plant industry classifications at the 4-digit level and even the 7-digit classification of the plant's primary product; see Section 4.A.3 on how this information was used in the construction of real variables.)

Table 4.8 records the distribution of the Primary Industry Specialization Ratio (PISR) across plant-year observations in the cleaned sample. The numbers indicate that production is extremely focused in most of the

Table 4.8: Primary industry specialization ratios

Percentile	PISR[a]
100	100 %
75	100 %
50	100 %
25	91 %
10	63 %
1	30 %
Plants	3014

Source: Longitudinal Research Database (LRD), U.S. Bureau of the Census; and own calculations.

[a] The primary industry specialization ratio is defined as the ratio of the output attributed to the plant's 4-digit SIC industry to total output. The 4-digit SIC code, in turn, is determined by the plant's primary product.

plants: For more than half of the observations, the PISR is 100 %, i. e., the plant's entire output can be attributed to a single 4-digit SIC industry. For less than 10 % of the observations, the PISR is below 63 %. This fact illustrates one of the major advantages of plant-level data: As output can be assigned to 4-digit SIC industries sharply, production and hence the production technology used in a given plant can be assumed to be rather homogenous. Also, output price indexes at the 4-digit SIC level can be used. These provide detailed information on demand movements (which can be heterogenous across industries and vary over time). These facts imply that heterogeneity problems (regarding production as well as demand) are alleviated by using such detailed plant-level information.

Next, I need to mention a sampling problem faced by all LRD users. As discussed in Section 4.A.1, not all small establishments (i. e., plants with less than 250 employees) are included in the LRD in non-Census years. (The Census of Manufactures is conducted only quinquennially.) As for this study, plant observations in consecutive years are required, so that such small plants cannot be included in the sample at all. This problem turned out not to be of great relevance for the study at hand because the firms considered are rather large and also have rather large plants (which can be checked for Census years in which all plants *are* covered). Also, as a general rule, once some firm has one plant selected for coverage in the non-Census years of the LRD, all its plants are included, even if they would have been too small to be selected individually. Based on the Census year coverage, I could verify that the coverage of plants for the 40 firms in the sample is almost complete, and missing plant years are due to administrative rather than sampling problems.

Table 4.9: Distribution of firm-level financial status[a]

Financial status	Kaplan-Zingales sample		Sample matched with LRD data[b]	
Not or likely not constrained	19	38.8 %	16	40.0 %
Possibly constrained	8	16.3 %	24	60.0 %
Likely or definitely constrained	22	44.9 %		
Total	49		40	

Source: Kaplan and Zingales (1997), Appendix; Longitudinal Research Database (LRD), U.S. Bureau of the Census; and own calculations.

[a] The financial constraints status reported in this table is Kaplan and Zingales's classification of firms for the entire sample period, not the annual indicator variable used elsewhere in this study.

[b] Due to disclosure restrictions, values for some individual cells based on LRD plant-level data cannot be reported; these cells have been collapsed pairwise in this table.

The original Kaplan-Zingales firm-level sample contains 49 firms with 729 firm-year observations for 1970–84.[56] As the annual coverage of the LRD starts in 1972, the sample period for the plant-level data is shorter, covering 13 years instead of 15. Table 4.9 reports the results of the matching process, in particular, the distribution of the financial constraints variable in the full sample with 49 firms and among the 40 firms for which LRD plant information was available. It is regrettable that the small sample of 49 firms was further reduced to only 40 firms, but the resulting sample still has (roughly) the same proportions of firms classified by Kaplan and Zingales as financially constrained and not constrained, respectively. Although I am unable to report further details due to disclosure restrictions, this observation suggests that the resulting sample still has enough variation in its yearly financial constraints indicator.

[56] Six firm-year observations (for two firms that entered the panel after 1970) are missing in their data, see Table 4.2.

Table 4.10: Plant operating status and firm-level financial status

KZI	Total		Operating		Not operating[a] Total		Idle	Sold	Closed
0	1976	65.6 %	1854	65.4 %	122	68.5 %	30	74	18
1	651	21.6 %	622	21.9 %	29	16.3 %	7	17	5
2	196	6.5 %	182	6.4 %	14	7.9 %			
3	102	3.4 %	94	3.3 %	8	4.5 %			
4	89	3.0 %	84	3.0 %	5	2.8 %			
Total	3014	100.0 %	2836	100.0 %	178	100.0 %			

Source: Kaplan and Zingales (1997), Appendix; Longitudinal Research Database (LRD), U.S. Bureau of the Census; and own calculations.

[a] Due to disclosure restrictions, values for some individual cells based on LRD plant-level data cannot be reported.

This can be seen from Table 4.10, where the distribution of plant-year observations across operating status and financial status is detailed. Note that this table contains *all* plant-year observations in the sample; one can see that there is a slight tendency for idle plants and exits (i. e., closures or sell-offs) to concentrate in years with a more constrained financial status. This fact is exploited by the econometric estimation exercises reported below, where exit decisions are shown to depend, after controlling for productivity and expected demand effects, on financial constraints.

Table 4.11: Correlations among alternative measures of firms' financial status

		correlation	P-value
Kaplan-Zingales indicator	vs. Debt-assets ratio	0.1678	0.0010
Kaplan-Zingales indicator	vs. Cash flow-assets ratio	-0.1782	0.0005
Cash flow-assets ratio	vs. Debt-assets ratio	-0.2316	0.0000

Source: Kaplan and Zingales (1997), Appendix; NBER Manufacturing Masterfile; and own calculations.

Notes: Correlations are based on all firm years in the estimation sample; if the (ordinal) Kaplan-Zingales financial constraints indicator variable is included, Spearman's rank correlation coefficient is reported.

Finally, Table 4.11 contains correlation coefficients of the financial constraints indicator constructed by Kaplan and Zingales and other variables typically considered in theoretical and empirical studies on the effects of firms' financial situation on their investment decisions (computed for the 40 firm sample over the entire 1972–84 period). As can be seen from the table, the correlations are far from perfect, which suggests that the Kaplan and Zingales variable indeed contains information other than that used in standard models. The correlations, however, have the expected sign: If anything, high-leverage firms tend to be classified by Kaplan and Zingales as being financially constrained and firms with large cash flows tend to be classified as not being constrained.

4.5 A reduced-form model of plant growth and exit

The reduced-form model of plant growth presented in this section is intended as a simple empirical framework to analyze the implications of standard intertemporal optimization models of plant dynamics discussed in Section 2.1. It allows us to investigate the determinants of plant growth, including financial status at the firm level, while at the same time controlling for plant exit, using the standard sample selection framework introduced by Heckman (1976, 1979).

Heckman's two-step model perhaps the most basic attempts to address the selection problem in applied econometric work. There are now many more sophisticated models available, and Heckman's model was chosen mainly for its simplicity and its intuitive appeal, not because it represents the best current effort in reduced-form selection bias correction. Note that the (structural) dynamic programming model of joint investment and exit decisions presented below avoids survival biases by construction; therefore, it represents a very powerful alternative to reduced-form correction of selection problems. By no means, therefore, is the comparison of Heckman's simple reduced-form model with a sophisticated structural model a fair "horse race".[57]

---

[57] An overview of more recent reduced-form methods for sample selection models can be found in Verbeek and Nijman (1996). In the context of a firm growth/exit model, Hall (1987) discusses the estimation of the parameters of the two-equation model using maximum likelihood methods. This is a modern and more powerful alternative to the model presented here.

The model consists of two equations, a plant exit equation and a plant growth equation:

$$I(\text{exit}_{it}) = \text{Prob}(x'_{it}\beta_1) + \mu_{1it}, \tag{4.1}$$

$$\text{growth}_{it} = x'_{it}\beta_2 + \sigma_{12}\frac{\phi(x'_{it}\hat{\beta}_1)}{1 - \Phi(x'_{it}\hat{\beta}_1)} + \mu_{2it}. \tag{4.2}$$

The explanatory variables are collected, together with a constant, in the vector x; they are the same in both equations (and will be detailed shortly). The growth equation also has the inverse Mill's ratio as a right-hand side variable, which allows to control for the probability of exit in a given plant year; $\phi(\cdot)$ and $\Phi(\cdot)$ are the p.d.f. and c.d.f. of the normal distribution, respectively. The plant exit equation is formulated as a binary probit model, while the growth equation is estimated using OLS. Hall (1987) contains a detailed discussion of the properties of the simultaneous plant growth/exit model. It should be noted that identification of the parameters in the two-equation system given by (4.1) and (4.2) relies on the non-linearity (in x) of the Mill's ratio that enters (4.2) as an additional regressor (and on the assumption that the errors μ_{1i} and μ_{2i} are jointly normally distributed, which is essentially untestable). In general, identification could also be achieved by imposing some exclusion restriction on either equation. In the application considered here, however, the underlying model of firm growth and exit implies that the driving forces of growth and exit are the same.

The plant growth rate is computed as the growth rate of plant output. As suggested by standard models of plant growth and exit discussed in Section 2.1, the right-hand side variables included in the reduced-form estimation are the existing capital stock (as a proxy for plant size), plant age, and relative plant productivity. Also, I include the capital-labor ratio to control for differences in production technology. Finally, the standard plant-level growth/exit model is amended with various measures of firm-level financial status to test whether firm-level finance affects plant-level decisions.

The productivity index used in the growth/exit model is defined as the residual from an auxiliary production function regression with capital, labor, and materials as inputs, and with time index to capture technical progress. Hence, productivity here is actually *relative* productivity (relative to the industry mean). This concept has been used widely in the plant-level productivity research (see, *inter alia*, Baily *et al.* (1992), Doms *et al.* (1995), and Olley and Pakes (1996)). The system of equations for this model is completed with the following auxiliary equation for plant productivity:

$$y_{it} = \beta_0^c + \beta_0^t t + \beta_0^k k_{it} + \beta_0^l l_{it} + \beta_0^m m_{it} + \sum_{j,k} \beta_0^{jk} X_{jkt} + \epsilon_{it}\,, \qquad (4.3)$$

where X_{jkt} denotes the cross products of the production factors. The results of alternative production function specifications are contained in Table 4.12. Generally, signs and magnitudes of the coefficients of the production functions are as expected (according to standard applied production analysis). The specification used to construct the productivity index is reported in the last column.

Table 4.12: Plant-level production function equations (OLS estimates)

Specification	Cobb-Douglas		Translog I		Translog II	
Constant	0.157	(0.55)	0.213	(0.76)	-0.131	(-0.68)
Time	0.018	(4.89)	0.017	(4.60)	0.015	(6.22)
Capital, K	0.170	(13.93)	0.253	(15.58)	-0.068	(-4.68)
Labor, L	0.689	(44.84)	0.711	(38.15)	0.496	(25.28)
Materials, M					0.520	(29.48)
$K \times K$			0.035	(4.45)	-0.012	(-2.05)
$L \times L$			0.048	(4.32)	0.090	(8.91)
$M \times M$					0.045	(5.84)
$K \times L$					-0.024	(-1.79)
$K \times M$					0.057	(5.09)
$L \times M$					-0.156	(-11.86)
Observations	3014		3014		3014	
Total SS	5451.3		5451.3		5451.3	
Residual SS	1297.9		1256.8		578.6	
R^2	0.762		0.769		0.894	
Probability of F-Test	0.000		0.000		0.000	

Source: Longitudinal Research Database (LRD), U.S. Bureau of the Census; and own calculations.
Note: t-values in parentheses. The regressions also contain industry dummies; parameter estimates for these are not reported here.

Tables 4.13 and 4.14 contain the estimation results of the plant exit and growth equations, respectively. Generally, the estimation of the parameters in both equations turned out to be relatively precise. The findings of the reduced-form plant-growth model are consistent with results reported in earlier studies: Small and highly productive plants tend to grow faster; however, the productivity variable does not have a significant effect on the exit decision.

Table 4.13: Plant exit equations (Probit estimates)

Specification	I		II		III	
Constant	-2.070	(-20.92)	-2.020	(-19.30)	-1.812	(-10.58)
Capital	-0.008	(-3.49)	-0.008	(-3.61)	-0.007	(-3.12)
Plant age	0.026	(3.51)	0.025	(3.35)	0.018	(2.39)
Productivity	-0.017	(-0.16)	-0.019	(-0.18)	-0.027	(-0.24)
Capital-labor ratio	0.094	(4.72)	0.095	(4.75)	0.083	(4.08)
Kaplan-Zingales indicator			-0.064	(-1.34)	-0.110	(-2.16)
Debt-assets ratio					0.284	(1.16)
Cash flow-assets ratio					-0.978	(-2.82)
Observations	3014		3014		3014	
Log likelihood	-517.7		-516.9		-510.6	
Likelihood ratio χ^2	35.93		37.80		50.48	
Probability of LR test	0.000		0.000		0.000	

Source: Longitudinal Research Database (LRD), U.S. Bureau of the Census; and own calculations.
Note: t-values in parentheses.

Turning to the financial variables, the central result is that plants owned by constrained firms (identified by the Kaplan-Zinagles indicator) tend to grow slower. The significance of the other financial variables in growth equations of this type varies with the particular specification, which is not surprising given their correlation structure reported earlier. A more detailed analysis of the impact of financial constraints on exit decisions is presented next with the structural estimation of the discrete dynamic programming model of joint investment and exit decisions.

Table 4.14: Plant growth equations (OLS estimates)

Specification	I		II		III	
Constant	0.263	(8.21)	0.280	(7.76)	0.152	(2.58)
Capital	0.000	(0.38)	0.001	(0.58)	-0.000	(-0.02)
Plant age	-0.005	(-1.51)	-0.007	(-2.18)	-0.005	(-1.97)
Productivity	0.185	(8.22)	0.183	(8.13)	0.186	(8.34)
Capital-labor ratio	-0.021	(-1.24)	-0.027	(-1.70)	-0.019	(-1.46)
Kaplan-Zingales indicator			-0.036	(-3.11)	-0.026	(-1.87)
Debt-assets ratio					0.057	(0.99)
Cash flow-assets ratio					0.341	(3.19)
Mills ratio	-1.162	(-1.58)	-0.846	(-1.21)	-0.904	(-1.47)
Observations	3014		3014		3014	
Total SS	695.6		695.6		695.6	
Residual SS	656.1		654.4		643.6	
R^2	0.057		0.059		0.075	
Probability of F-Test	0.000		0.000		0.000	

Source: Longitudinal Research Database (LRD), U.S. Bureau of the Census; and own calculations.
Note: t-values in parentheses.

4.6 Empirical results for the structural model of investment and exit

4.6.1 Estimation of the dynamic programming model

The dynamic programming model of joint investment and market exit decisions at the plant level is discussed in detail in Section 3.3. Recall that the model has two control variables: For each plant, firms decide at the beginning of each period whether to continue operating (the exit decision), and if so, how much to invest. These decisions are made given current state variables and under rational expectations over future state variables (reflecting, for example, expectations about future prices and demand). For estimation, the investment variable is discretized. This allows the use of a modified version of Rust's (1987) nested fixed-point algorithm described in Section 3.2.3.

Structural assumptions

The following structural assumptions are made to make the model presented in Section 3.3.1 tractable. The per-period profit function $\Pi(\cdot)$ is given by gross revenue (i. e., the total value of production determined by the production function) less variable factor costs (with labor and materials as variable factors) and capital stock adjustment costs:

$$\begin{aligned}\Pi(s,a) &= r(s,a) - c(s,a) \\ &= pf(k,l,m) - p^l l - p^m m - p^k c(i)\,. \end{aligned} \tag{4.4}$$

Here, $r(\cdot)$ is per-period net revenue (i.e., gross revenue, or, at the plant level, the value of shipments less operation and variable factor costs), $c(\cdot)$ is the cost of adjusting the plant's capital stock according to the optimal decision rule[58], and $f(\cdot)$ is the production function. Prices for outputs and inputs are given by p, p^l, p^m, and p^k, respectively; they are assumed to be determined on perfectly competitive markets. Assuming that the decision to shut down the plant has no cost by itself, and that capital stock adjustment costs are a function of investment, one can write $c(s,a) = p^k c(i)$. In the empirical application, the production function that determines the value of plant production is assumed to be Cobb-Douglas, with capital, labor, and materials as inputs. Capital stock adjustment costs $c(i)$ are modeled as a quadratic function of gross investment.

The important point to note here is that this model of firm investment and exit decisions is a special case of the DDP framework derived in Section 3.1.3, so the numerical solution methods and the econometric estimation methods derived in Sections 3.2.3 apply. The parameters of interest that are estimated in the empirical application are, first, the parameters of the Cobb-Douglas production function, and second, the parameters of the partial likelihood functions for the two decision variables, (discretized) investment and exit.

Financial constraints enter the structural model via an additional state variable, the firm's financial status. This firm-level variable is assumed to be exogenous at the plant-level. This approach is motivated by the discussion in Section 3.1.4 and the modeling approach by Hajivassiliou

---

[58] In slight abuse of notation, $c(s,a)$ is in nominal terms, while $c(i)$ is in real terms, with $p^k c(i)$ denoting nominal costs of adjustment.

and Ioannides (1994). Recall that the financial status variable is recorded at the firm level and assumed to be exogenous at the plant level. In the dynamic discrete-choice model, financial constraints at the firm level affect discrete plant-level decisions via the second-stage partial likelihoods given by (3.26). If the financial status variable were modeled as being endogenous, it would also enter the first-stage partial likelihoods (3.25) that reflect the agent's beliefs about the evolution of state variables. However, experimentation with the current model and the data set at hand has shown that, empirically, the link between plant-level state variables and firm-level financial status is too weak to allow the estimation of such a relationship.

Implementation of the NFXP algorithm

The estimation of the model parameters was performed using a version of the nested fixed-point algorithm described in Section 3.2.3. The software was adapted from the original Gauss code for Rust's (1987) bus motor replacement problem (a detailed documentation can be found in Rust (1995)). Recall that the decision problem in that application was whether to replace a bus motor or not given its accumulated mileage at the beginning of each period; thus the original code was written for just one discrete control and one continuous state variable. However, given the matrix-oriented nature of Gauss, adapting the code for the case of more control and state variables is straightforward. Some concepts used in the resulting modifications are based on Rust's Fortran code for his series of papers on retirement decisions which have multiple control and state variables. These papers are Rust (1989, 1990, 1992) and, in particular, the two-control-variable model of retirement and social security acceptance decisions by Rust and Phelan (1997).

Estimation was performed on a Hewlett-Packard HP 9000-730 workstation with 80 Megabyte of core memory. A single run of the inner loop, i. e., finding a solution the full DP model presented in Section 3.3.1 for a given set of parameters, requires between 30 and 240 seconds of CPU time, depending on the number of state variables and the discretization used. For convergence of the modified BHHH optimization algorithm used in the outer loop, between 10 and 30 iterations were necessary (typically, the maximum number of iterations was set to 30 before or the estimation was aborted), a typical number for a non-linear ML model.

Some versions of the model did not converge at all, and in these cases, the problem was mainly related to the imprecise estimation of the discount rate. Ultimately, the discount rate was fixed at a value of $\beta = 0.97$, corresponding to an annual risk-free rate of about 3.1 %. Fixing the discount factor to improve the convergence of the iterative maximum likelihood estimator is common practice in NFXP applications (e. g., in the study by Rust and Phelan (1997), the discount factor was fixed as well).[59] Given these timings, a few specifications of the investment/exit model can be run in a single overnight job. It is clear, however, that even slight increases in the dimension of the state space would effectively prevent estimating the model with the current Gauss software on a fast workstation.

It should be noted that the size of the dataset (i.e., the number of plant-year observations) is not relevant for the time required to solve the DP problem; the data only enter the outer (maximum likelihood) loop of the estimation algorithm. Given the size of core memory available when working on this study, much larger datasets could have been used without a major increase in estimation time. In fact, the computational burden induced by the size of the dataset is dominated by the burden of solving the DP problem in most economic applications (which tend to have rather small datasets compared with other sciences).

Estimation results

The structural estimation of the dynamic programming model is in fact a maximum likelihood estimation of the model's deep (technology) parameters which enter primarily the profit function $\Pi(\cdot)$ (with the production function assumed to be of the Cobb-Douglas type). These estimates are not by themselves informative for the problem at hand – they are time-invariant deep parameters which can be used to analyze intertemporal choices under rational expectations consistently. Other estimated parameters are essentially void of an economic interpretation and the results are omitted here. Such nuisance parameters are, e. g., the the scale factors that reflect time-varying interest rates. Note also that the estimated

[59] As discussed in Section 3.3.2, fixing the discount rate amounts to the assumption that there is a fixed risk-free interest rate and shifting the time-varying component of the interest rate into the value function where it is treated as a macroeconomic state variable.

model reflects the decision maker's expectations about the plant's future profitability (as captured by the profit function).

Table 4.15: Implicit choice probabilities (nested fixed-point algorithm)

Decision	Exit		Zero investment	
Intercept	-1.893	(-19.24)	1.531	(29.58)
Capital	-0.006	(-2.58)	-0.000	(-0.06)
Plant age	0.025	(3.37)	0.015	(3.99)
Productivity	-0.016	(-0.15)	-0.113	(-2.07)
Kaplan-Zingales indicator	-0.059	(-1.27)	0.690	(3.24)

Source: Longitudinal Research Database (LRD), U.S. Bureau of the Census; and own calculations.
Note: t-values in parentheses.

Based on the estimates of the deep parameters, it is possible to compute the parameters of the logit models associated with the two binary choices. Results for two discrete decisions are reported in Table 4.15. In the structural model, attention is restricted to the financial status variable by Kaplan and Zingales because the model requires to specify a single state variable reflecting firm-level financial status. The finding here is consistent with that of the reduced-form model: Financially constrained firms tend to close plants more often, given their expectations about future profitability (which are captured by the intertemporal optimization framework). Capital stock (i. e., the size of the plant) and plant age have negative signs in the exit equation, a finding which is again consistent with results in similar studies such as Olley and Pakes (1996). The intertemporal optimization model also confirms that financially constrained firms are more likely to chose zero investment at the plant level, after controlling for profitability and endogenous exit decisions. This result supports the view that the financial status of a firm affects its investment behavior (in this case, as observed at the plant level).

4.6.2 Removing financial constraints: a policy simulation

The policy experiment made here is to remove the financial constraints entirely by setting the corresponding state variable to the unconstrained value for all plants and periods, $f_t^i = 0$, $t = 1973, \ldots, 1984$. Then, given the true (observed) values for the other state variables and the same process of exogenous variables such as input and output prices, the model is re-solved and the corresponding stochastic process $\{\tilde{s}_t, \tilde{a}_t\}_{1973}^{1984}$ is computed. Note that by construction, this simulated stochastic process evolves differently from the observed process that was used for estimation, $\{s_t, a_t\}$. Given the results of the structural estimation of the choice probabilities for the discrete exit and investment decision variables, it should not come as a surprise that both the number of zero investment observations and the number of exits in the simulated data decrease (from 130 exits in the observed data to 74 exits in the simulated data). These results imply that in the last period, 1984, the observed dataset has 314 plants, while the simulated dataset has 370 plants.

More striking, however, is the impact of removing all financial constraints on the growth process of plants: A useful way to assess the impact of this policy change on plant dynamics is to look at the distribution of plant size in the last period of both observed and simulated data. Figures 4.3 and 4.4 show non-parametrically estimated densities of the distributions of plant size.[60] The densities are estimated for the plants remaining in 1984 in the observed data (top panels) and in the simulated data (bottom panels). Figure 4.3 shows the distribution of real output, while Figure 4.4 shows real capital stocks. In both cases, the mass of the distribution is shifted to the right in the simulated data, indicating that without financial constraints, plants would have grown faster. Also, the simulated distributions have a lower variance because during the growth process that results in these distributions, plants are not subject to one class of shocks, the occasionally binding financial constraints.

One can only push these results so far, however, as removing financial constraints in this simulation exercise does not account for general equilibrium effects. If macroeconomic fluctuations are a central determinant of financial constraints and hence of the financial status indicator considered here, it is hard to think of a real world scenario that would correspond to a 13-year boom period without financial constraints. A second problem of this simulation is that endogenous entries cannot be generated

[60] The non-parametric density estimation was performed using a Gaussian kernel and the fast Fourier transformation method described by Silverman (1986), pp. 61–66. Bandwidth selection was by least-squares cross-validation. The estimation code is based on the Gauss routine `np_dens` written by Mico Loretan.

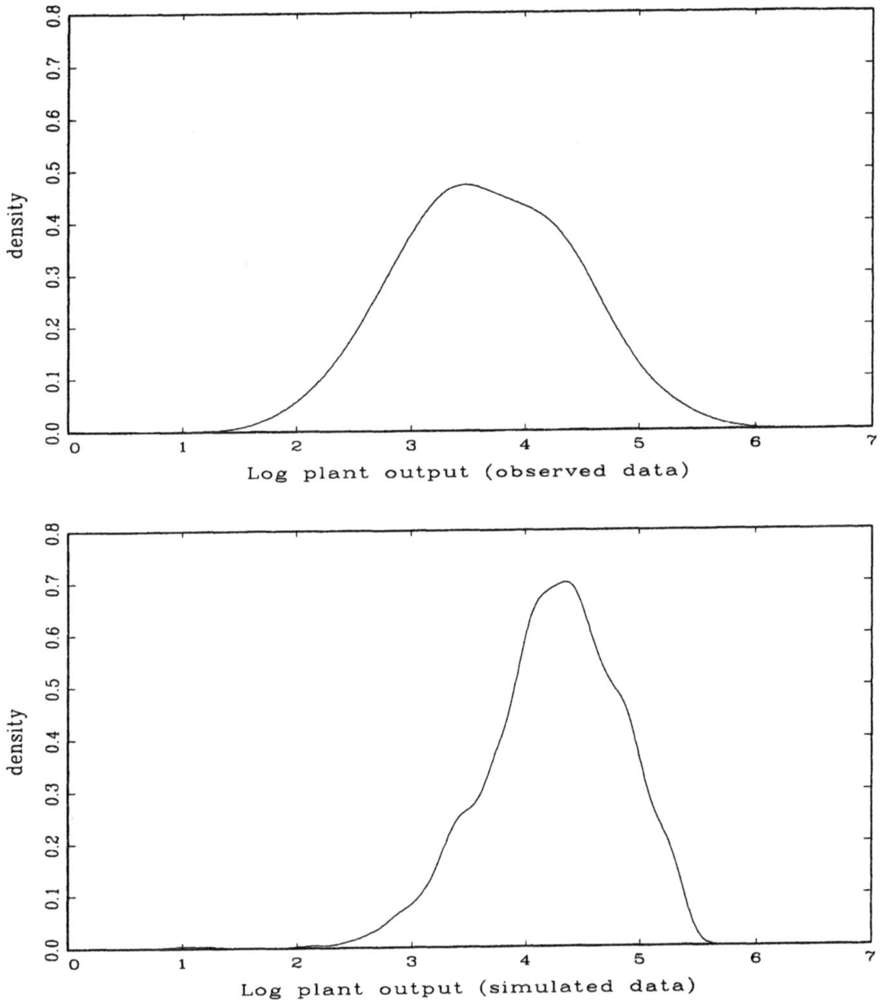

Figure 4.3: Smoothed plant output distributions for observed and simulated data, 1984

Source: Longitudinal Research Database (LRD), U.S. Bureau of the Census; and own calculations.

Notes: The top panel shows the distribution of the observed plant ouput, the bottom panel shows the distribution of the simulated plant output (where financial constraints were removed). The non-parametric densities were estimated using a Gaussian kernel smoother.

with the structural model at hand: While for the purpose of estimation, observed entries are not a problem because the determinants of entry do not affect the decision process of observed plants, it is conceivable that

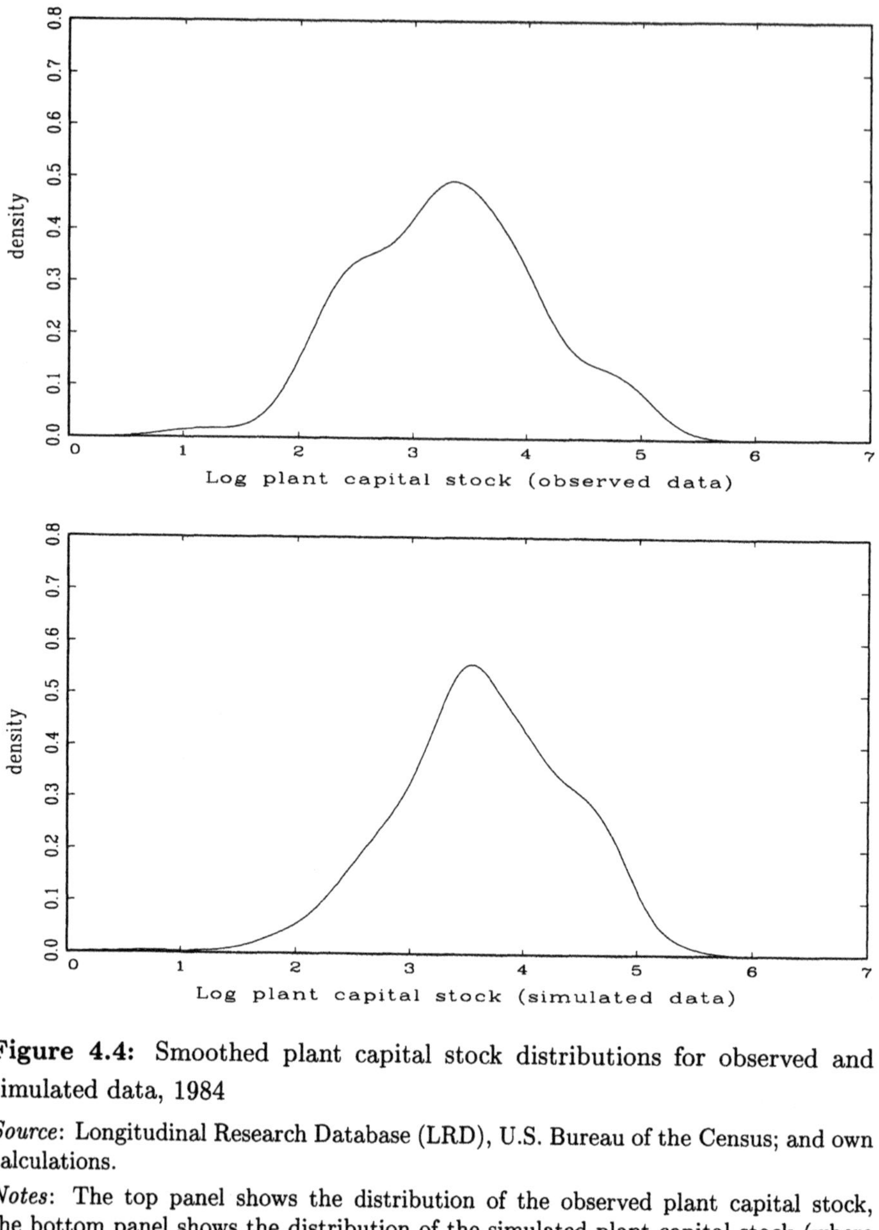

Figure 4.4: Smoothed plant capital stock distributions for observed and simulated data, 1984

Source: Longitudinal Research Database (LRD), U.S. Bureau of the Census; and own calculations.

Notes: The top panel shows the distribution of the observed plant capital stock, the bottom panel shows the distribution of the simulated plant capital stock (where financial constraints were removed). The non-parametric densities were estimated using a Gaussian kernel smoother.

better macroeconomic conditions and the absence of financial constraints would also generate more entries in the simulated data. However, note that this effect would only increase the size effect observed in the simulated data, so the (qualitative) simulation results remain valid and give a lower bound on the "true" size effects under the simulated policy.

Taken together, this policy simulation exercise does show how financial constraints influence plant-level investment and exit decisions and how they contribute to the dynamic evolution of the plant size distribution. Note also that a similar exercise could not have been performed using the reduced-form approach presented earlier: Only a structural model of plant investment can be re-solved for an alternative policy in order to simulate a new stochastic process $\{\tilde{s}_t, \tilde{a}_t\}$.

4.7 Summary and discussion

On balance, the empirical results reported in this chapter confirm the finding in much of the existing literature on the effects of financial constraints on investment: They exist. Here, this result was obtained using a new measure of the firm's financial status which reflects more information than simple sample-split approaches, and using a structural intertemporal optimization model of firm decisions that was designed to account for endogenous exit decisions, a problem usually ignored in similar studies. One of the strengths of the structural estimation approach presented in Section 4.6 is that it allows for valid policy simulations (in the sense that it is not subject to the *Lucas critique*). In this paper, I simulated the dynamics of investment and exit for a given initial distribution of plants under an alternative policy regime with no financial constraints at all. While such a regime is not conceivable in reality, the simulation results still show that financial constraints have dramatic effects on plant dynamics relative to a first-best world.

The model presented here surely has its limitations, the most serious of which is the exogeneity assumption imposed on the firm's financial situation in the empirical plant-level investment/exit model. Given the econometric techniques for intertemporal optimization models currently available, this was the only way make the model operational. Hence, this paper should be seen as a first step in this direction, showing that in principle, such an approach is practicable. In a more general model, one might wish to allow for, first, a richer decision space, both in terms of the number of choice variables available to the firm and a finer discretization of continuous choice variables, second, more state variables with a finer discretization, and third, more general forms of state transition dynamics (in particular, an endogenous financial status variable). All of these extensions, however, will increase the dimension of the dynamic programming problem and its computational complexity tremendously (this is Bellman's famous "curse of dimensionality"). In practice, the model presented here reaches the limits of the numerical capabilities of current standard workstations. I return to this issue in my concluding remarks (Chapter 5).

The second concern with the empirical implementation here is sample size. While the size of the sample is fairly large in terms of individual plants covered, the number of firms is small. This is mainly due to the fact that the financial constraints indicator had been constructed for a very small sample in the first place. Given that this indicator was shown to convey information about the firm's financial situation that is actually helpful in explaining investment and exit decisions, further research into such indicators seems warranted (and may lead to larger samples as well).

4.A Data appendix

The data used in this study for the empirical analysis of firms' investment decisions are mainly plant-level data collected by the U.S. Bureau of the Census through its (quinquennial) Census of Manufactures and its Annual Survey of Manufactures. These data are contained in a comprehensive database that covers a large part of U.S. manufacturing, the Longitudinal Research Database (LRD). In this study, plant-level data are linked with industry-level data on prices and depreciation rates and with firm-level data on the firms' financial status. The advantages of using disaggregated (i. e., plant-level) data in the empirical analysis of investment behavior have been highlighted in Section 2.1.4.

In this appendix, I discuss the data used in this study and their sources in detail. First, I present the Longitudinal Research Database and the sources of other data used (Section 4.A.1). In Section 4.A.2, I describe how plant and firm-level data are linked to form an unbalanced panel containing all plants for a pre-specified set of firms (or for some pre-specified industry, for that matter) and address potential selection problems that may arise in this process. Finally, I discuss the construction of the variables used for estimation, Section 4.A.3. Notes on the terminology of *plants* and *firms* as used in this study are contained in the Appendix 4.A.4.

4.A.1 Data sources

In this section, I discuss the sources of the data used in Chapter 4. First, I present details on the Longitudinal Research Database which is the source of all plant-level data; then I describe the sources of firm and industry-level data.

Plant-level data from the Longitudinal Research Database

The main source of data used in this study is the Longitudinal Research Database (LRD) maintained by the Center for Economic Studies (CES) at the U.S. Bureau of the Census, Washington, D.C.

The information on individual establishments contained in the LRD is confidential and protected by Title 13, U.S. Code, which specifies that the Census Bureau may not publish or release any data provided by individual respondents to censuses and other Census Bureau surveys. Hence, all work using LRD plant-level data has to be conducted on site at the CES, and all research output is reviewed by CES staff for violation of disclosure rules. In particular, these procedures are designed to ensure that no information on any individual plant or firm can be reconstructed from released research output. For a detailed description of the LRD, see McGuckin and Pascoe (1988) and the technical appendix in Davis *et al.* (1996). A report by the Center for Economic Studies (1992) discusses technical details of the database.

The LRD contains annual cost and output data on manufacturing establishments (plants) based on the quinquennial Census of Manufactures (CM) conducted in the years 1963, 1967, 1972, 1977, 1982, 1987, and 1992. For the remaining (henceforth, non-census) years since 1972, the LRD contains information obtained through the Annual Survey of Manufactures (ASM). The datafiles for the individual years can be linked to form an unbalanced longitudinal panel, with annual observations ranging from 1972 through, currently, 1993. The number of plants in the CM is about 300,000–400,000, covering all but the smallest manufacturing establishments in the U.S. In non-census years, data are available only for a probability sample of about 50,000–70,000 plants taken from the CM. While all large establishments (over 250 employees) are included in the ASM, smaller plants are included in the ASM panel with probability increasing with plant size. These establishments, in turn, are included only for five years; then, a new sample of ASM establishments is drawn for the next five years (resulting in a rotating five year panel). Hence, there are only few small establishments in consecutive AMS years. In general, this will lead to some selection biases for small establishments.[61] The degree to which this is a problem for this study is discussed in Section 4.4.

Sources of firm and industry-level data

In the empirical application contained in this study, LRD plant-level data were augmented with financial variables recorded at the firm level and with price data and depreciation rates recorded at the industry level.

---

[61] This fact is well known to other LRD users, see Caballero *et al.* (1997) for a detailed discussion.

For the set of firms identified as being financially constrained by Fazzari *et al.* (1988) and further investigated by Kaplan and Zingales (1997), the values of the annual financial status variable were taken *verbatim* from the appendix in Kaplan and Zingales (1997). Further details on the financial status variable can be found in Section 4.2. Other firm-level financial variables used in this study are based on publicly available balance-sheet information. They were extracted from the NBER Manufacturing Masterfile (see Hall (1990)) which in turn is based on firms' balance-sheet data contained in the Compustat database. All firm-level financial variables were matched with LRD plant-level variables using a name matching procedure.

In addition to firm-level financial data, a number of industry-specific variables were matched with the plant-year observations contained in the LRD-based unbalanced panel. The matching of industry-level data was based on the 4-digit industry classification for each plant, as contained in the LRD (or the 2-digit industry derived from the 4-digit industry).

Deflators for the various output and input measures used in this study are taken, at the 4-digit industry level, from the NBER Manufacturing Productivity Database (see Bartelsman and Gray (1994) for details). These annual deflators have 1987 as their base year, hence all real variables used in this study are expressed in terms of 1987 dollars. A slight complication arises from the fact that the NBER Productivity Database uses the 1972 version of the SIC while the LRD is based on the most recent 1987 SIC issue. In a number of cases, plants included in the dataset switched their assigned 4-digit industry as a result of the SIC revision; such changes have been taken care of when constructing the real variables used in this study. In most cases, there exists a simple one-to-one mapping from the 1987 4-digit SIC into the 1972 4-digit SIC; remaining ambiguities were resolved by going back to the 5-digit product class code of the plant's primary product (the latter is reported at the 7-digit level for each plant in the LRD).

The annual capital depreciation rates used for constructing capital stocks are based on the 2-digit industry level. They were obtained from the Bureau of Economic Analysis (BEA). The method used by BEA for constructing the underlying industry-specific capital input measures is, in turn, the same as that used by the Bureau of Labor Statistics in their productivity studies; see Hulten and Wykoff (1981), U.S. Bureau of Labor Statistics (1983) and U.S. Bureau of Economic Analysis (1984) for detailed discussions.

4.A.2 Building the raw panel

In the following, I describe the process of matching and merging the various data sources used in this study. This discussion does not only apply to the empirical application presented in this chapter; its purpose is to address some methodological and practical issues which emerge when constructing a dataset that contains both plant and firm-level data. To some degree, these issues are independent of the particular specification of the empirical model to be estimated.

For simplicity, I refer to the dataset only in an abstract sense as an (unbalanced) "panel", for a detailed discussion of selection criteria for the plants and firms covered by these datasets, see Section 4.4. Recall that the plants included in the estimation dataset were selected on the basis of a set of firms for which firm-level financial information is available (Step 1). Steps 2 and 3 amount to building an unbalanced panel from these plant observations and augmenting this panel with external information; these steps are essentially the same whether external firm-level information is used or not.

Step 1: Matching plant and firm-level observations

Assume for the moment that a panel of firm-level observations is given (for a specified set of firms and some sample period), consisting of one or more annual financial variable(s) and some header information identifying each firm. These firm-year observations are to be matched with corresponding plant-year observations from another source. Note that the number of plant-year observations matched to a firm-year observation may vary both over time and across firms.

In practice, the main complication for the matching of firm and plant datasets arises from the fact that there is no identifier available for firms which is universally used across different datasets. On the firm level, the identifier used in most balance-sheet based data sources such as Compustat or the NBER Manufacturing Sector Masterfile is the CUSIP number. However, this is not the identifier used by the Census Bureau, for obvious reasons: The scope of the Census of Manufactures is much wider and it is primarily plant-level based. Hence, the Census Bureau uses its own set of firm and plant identifiers which allow to track individual plants over time and across ownership changes. The matching of any external information with the LRD therefore relies primarily on the recorded firm names and string matching. Typing errors in the datasets, different versions and abbreviations of firm names, firms that change their name over time, or simply multiple occurances of firm names make this matching process tedious and in most cases result in a less than full matching. For larger datasets, the amount of additional work required to resolve critical cases can be prohibitive. Another reason for unsuccessful matches is that the LRD is restricted to manufacturing, so there is no plant-level information for firms with mainly non-manufacturing output.

In practice, a list of the firm names for which financial variables are available were fed into a name-matching process to identify plants covered by the LRD which were owened by the firms on the list. This matching process started with the Census years 1972, 1977, 1982 and 1987, because only in Census years are all manufacturing plants covered by the LRD. Based on the successful matches, lists containing the internal LRD plant identifiers were used to extract plant-year observations for the non-Census (ASM) years. As noted above, the number of establishments covered by the ASM is much smaller than the number of establishments in the LRD, but for the applications presented below a rather large fraction of plants contained in Census years also appeared in ASM years. In most cases these plants were larger than the 250 employee cut-off size for ASM years. This is an important size effect: firms for which financial data are available are larger and tend to have larger plants as well.

A first note on selection biases

At this point, it should be noted that the firm-plant matching approach used for the construction of any dataset involving external financial information might result in sample selection biases from three sources. First, starting from a pre-specified set of firms for which external financial information is available, there remains usually a subset of firms for which no plants can be found in the LRD (as a consequence of the name-matching process). It is, however, reasonable to assume that these non-matches occur randomly. However, a much more important second selection mechanism is related to the size effect just mentioned: Financial information is available only for a non-random subsample of firms in the first place (for example, for firms listed on the stock exchange which, in turn, tend to be larger). Finally, plant-level information might not be available for firms in the pre-specified set that primarily operate in non-manufacturing industries (even if they have some manufacturing activities at some establishment).

Step 2: Deriving an unbalanced panel from plant-level data

The LRD is the source of all plant-level variables used in this study, such as output, investment, and other input measures. Information contained in the LRD is also used to identify plant entries and exits and to characterize their nature. The central step of the data merging process takes the definition of the cross-sectional dimension of the sample (either just SIC codes or the list of successful matches obtained in Step 1) as its input and extracts the required variables from separate annual LRD files for all years in the sample. This results in an unbalanced panel consisting of, say, annual output, investment and other input variables, industry and product classifiers, and – in the case of a panel entry or exit in a given year – a variable indicating the nature of that event, i.e. whether

- a *panel entry* is a newly opened plant, related to an ownership change, or due to the sampling procedure for small plants in the ASM years (as described above), and
- a *panel exit* is a plant closure, an ownership change, or due to sampling.

Concentrating on the longitudinal dimension of the unbalanced panel, an important issue is the number of adjacent plant-year observations required for the econometric estimation of a given model. The need for such a longitudinal dimension in the dataset arises whenever an empirical investigation is based on intertemporal optimization behavior (as is the case in this study). Empirical models which account for endogenous entry and exit allow for unbalanced panels; this helps to avoid selection biases – and usually results in considerably increased sample sizes.[62] Even when unbalanced panels are used, the need for sufficiently long observed

[62] It is therefore unfortunate when limitations of estimation procedures prevent researchers from using unbalanced panels: Not only does this introduce particular

spells can reduce the sample size considerably; moreover, it can introduce particular forms of selection bias.

A second note on selection biases

At this point, it is useful to address some selection problems of the LRD plant-level database which are due to the sampling scheme for small plants in ASM (non-Census) years. Observations on small plants (i. e., with less than 250 employess) which are covered by the LRD only in Census years, but not in ASM years, cannot be used in the panel because information is available only in five-year intervals.[63] This issue is not of particular relevance for the empirical application presented in Chapter 4, as the size effect introduced by matching external financial data reduces the scope for small plants from the outset. It turned out that for these datasets, only very few plants selected in Census years had subsequently to be discarded because they were not included in the ASM years.

Two other sampling issues are the length of observed plant spells and left truncation. The latter issue refers to the fact that no information is available on plants for the years before 1972, making it difficult to estimate any model that conditions current behavior on past observed variables, at least for the first few years in the panel. Generally, left truncation would imply that the information on early exits (i. e., exits observed in the first few years of the panel) is insufficient, resulting in selection biases if such short, left-truncated spells were dropped.

A related problem arises for the probability sample of small plants that are included in the five-year rotating ASM panels. For example, consider observations on small plants which were only sampled for one ASM rotating panel, resulting in five consecutive years of data. If there is a missing value in some of these five years, the observed spells might be too short to allow estimation using models which allow for serial dependence of some variables (e. g., the error term). Further, theory suggests that

---

selection biases (see the discussion in Section 2.1), it would also reduce the sample size even if entries and exits were independent of the economic phenomenon under investigation.

63 Some reduced-form plant-growth regressions use growth rates that are calculated over longer periods, controlling for exits with a separate equation estimated on the full observed sample in the initial year (e. g., Doms *et al.* (1995)). Such an approach could, in principle, use all CM plants for estimation.

exits are more likely for young firms, hence exits should frequently be associated with short observed spells (not independently of plant size, of course). In the case of plant exit after a very short observed spell, the loss of observations might result in a selection bias for exiting plants. Again, this bias is exacerbated for small plants by the ASM sampling scheme which restricts observed spells for most small plants to five years at most.

A Markovian structure reduces these biases because even short observed plant spells can be used. It allows to use plant-year observations even if there are only two adjacent years available for a given plant. For the same reason, missing data in a single plant-year observation are less of a problem, too. There is less need to impute these missing values, as in most cases dropping such an observation leaves the remaining years in the sample. Hence, the Markovian structure of the model allows for larger sample sizes and better coverage of plant exits, in particular for smaller plants. It also helps to reduce some forms of selection bias. A Markovian structure might be criticized because it restricts the patterns of serial correlations of both observed and unobserved state variables, but is has major practical advantages for panel studies, in particular given the sampling structure of the LRD.[64]

The distribution of plant spells in the resulting unbalanced panel is analyzed below (see Table 4.6); they range from 1 to 12 years, with a considerable fraction of short spells that would have been more difficult to handle in non-Markovian set-ups. Note that these figures already exclude the first year of each observed plant spell as that was used to construct the state variables for the first year used in estimation.

Step 3: Adding non-LRD data at the firm and industry levels

In the final step of the data merging process, the unbalanced panel constructed from LRD plant-level data is augmented with firm and industry-level data from various other sources. This is now straightforward, as firm-plant matches have been recorded in Step 1, and industry-level variables can be matched using the plants' 4-digit SIC classification contained in the LRD.

---

[64] Also, even though the assumption of a Markovian decision process is strong, it can be tested, as discussed in Section 3.2.3.

The resulting unbalanced raw panel

The output of the plant selection, matching and merging process for plant, firm and industry data described in Steps 1, 2, and 3 is an unbalanced panel that serves as the input for the construction of the model variables. I take up that issue in the next section. Note that the panel is unbalanced in many dimensions: Individual plants may have different entry and exit dates even if owned by one firm, while firms differ in the number of owned plants contained in the panel. As a result, the first and last years for which some plant is observed vary across firms as well.

4.A.3 Construction of model variables

A typical plant-year observation in the unbalanced panel used for estimation of the discrete dynamic programming model is a (row) vector of length $|X| + |A| + |O|$ and contains the following variables:

- Observable state variables, $x_t^i \in X$, at the plant or firm level:
  capital stock
  plant age
  financial status

- Decision variables, $a_t^i \in A$, at the plant level:
  a discrete operating status decision
  a discrete investment decision

- Other variables entering the profit function, o_t^i, at the plant level:
  labor input
  materials input
  output

Note that all other variables, such as firm characteristics (e.g., SIC product codes) and industry prices, are not elements of this vector, but have been used to construct these variables – only those variables which are part of the underlying optimization problem are actually used in the structural estimation. Next, I describe the construction of each of these variables in detail.

Discrete operating decision The LRD contains detailed information on the operating status of a given plant in each year. In particular, this "coverage code" allows to identify plants that were closed permanently or experienced ownership changes. According to the coverage code, each plant-year observation was assigned one of the values normal operation, idle, sold, or closed. Table 4.16 contains further details.

Table 4.16: Definition of the discrete operating status variable

Category	Operating status	Plants[a]	
0	Plant in normal operation (positive output)	395	68.9 %
1	Plant idle (zero output)	48	8.4 %
2	Plant sold	100	17.5 %
3	Plant permanently closed	30	5.2 %
Total		573	

Source: Longitudinal Research Database (LRD), U.S. Bureau of the Census; and own calculations.

[a] Last observed year of each plant spell.

Real investment The investment variable is constructed by adding the LRD variables for equipment and structures investment. Conversion to 1987 Dollars uses the deflators discussed above.

Real capital stock The capital stock measures are constructed for equipment capital and building structures separately; only after all the following adjustments have been made are these two components added to yield a single real capital stock variable. Initial capital stocks (used in the first year a plant is observed in the sample) are constructed from the book values reported in the LRD. For the remaining years, a perpetual inventory method with time-varying annual depreciation factors is used. This method is considered to be more reliable than the standard approach which amounts to picking a more or less arbitrary depreciation rate (such as, say, 10 %) and leaving it constant over time and across industries. Conversion to 1987 Dollars uses the deflators discussed above.

Plant age For plants that were established after 1972, age (in years) is straightforward to construct. For older plants (i. e., plants observed in the LRD in 1972 and not reported to be newly established in that year), the LRD records for the years 1963 and 1967 were checked. If a plant was already in operation in these years, it is classified as being 10 or 5 years old, respectively, in 1972. This method reduces the bias introduced by left-truncation of plant histories, but of course cannot remove it entirely.

Financial status variables These firm-level variables are taken *verbatim* from Kaplan and Zingales (1997, Appendix), and from the NBER Manufacturing Masterfile.

Real output and real variable factor inputs These variables are constructed from the respective nominal LRD variables, applying the standard variable definitions used by LRD researchers. They are then converted to 1987 Dollars using the deflators discussed above. Plant-level output is defined as the total value of shipments, adjusted for inventory changes.

4.A.4 A note on terminology

Company The definition used by the U.S. Bureau of the Census for the concept of a *company* is somewhat different from standard use.[65] To avoid potential confusion, the term *company* is not used throughout this study; for its purpose, the concept of the *firm* is sufficient.

Establishment See *plant*.

Firm A *firm* is an enterprise, that is, all establishments with common ownership.[66] Note that this concept of the firm is used exclusively in this study.

Plant A *plant* (or *establishment*) is a business or industrial unit at a single physical location which produces or distributes goods, or performs services. When more than one company conducts operations at a single location, each business under separate ownership is regarded as a separate

[65] The Census Bureau defines a *company* as a "business organization consisting of one or more establishments under common ownership ***which produce the same primary output***" (Center for Economic Studies (1992), this author's emphasis). Outside the Census Bureau, the term ***line of business*** is used for this concept. Note also that the Census Bureau's concept of a *company* is different from the concept of a *firm*.

[66] This definition is the one used by the U.S. Bureau of the Census, taken from Center for Economic Studies (1992).

establishment. Also, if a company engages in several distinctively different kinds of economic activity at one location, each activity is treated as a separate establishment if the separate activities are economically significant in size and if separate records are available.[67]

Manufacturing sector The empirical part of this study – due to the availability of data in the LRD – restricts attention to plants which belong to the manufacturing sector, i. e., to product groups 20–39 of the Standard Industrial Classification (SIC).

[67] This definition is similar to the one used by the U.S. Bureau of the Census, as stated in Center for Economic Studies (1992).

Chapter 5

Concluding remarks

The main purposes of this study were first, to develop a flexible empirical framework that allows to test the implications of different aspects of the more recent investment literature, and second, to present an empirical application that illustrates the advantages of this approach. The framework chosen was that of (discrete) Markov decision processes, for two main reasons. As discussed in Section 3.1, this framework is very flexible. It allows, for example, to incorporate various non-standard constraints into models of firm behavior, related to both "real" and "financial" aspects of investment decisions. Also, there are powerful methods available for structural econometric estimation of discrete decision processes; these were discussed in Section 3.2. These tools were put to work in an empirical model of firms' investment and exit decisions in Section 3.3, and in Chapter 4, I presented an empirical application of this model (extended to allow for financial constraints).

These concluding remarks address the two central results of this study, one essentially methodological, the other empirical. First, I discuss the usefulness of Markov decision processes as a framework for empirical studies of intertemporal economic decisions under uncertainty. Second, I show that these advantages are not only interesting from a methodological point of view, but that they also carry over to an empirical application, namely an investigation of firms' investment behavior under financial constraints. Finally, I address the major practical problem associated with structural estimation of dynamic decision processes: The computational requirements have prevented widespread use of these methods so far, and they also restrict the specification of the empirical model used in this study. There is, however, the hope that a combination of more refined estimation algorithms and more powerful hardware will push the frontier of models that are actually amenable to structural econometric estimation further out.

The usefulness of Markov decision processes in empirical work

The main appeal of the Markov decision process (MDP) framework is its flexibility. In a sense, the MDP framework is too flexible, because in principle, any observed intertemporal decision behavior can be rationalized by some MDP. However, if one takes a more constructive view, the researcher's goal is to build parsimonious models of intertemporal choice which yield optimal policies that are consistent with observed behavior. As I have shown in Chapter 3, there are many examples for successful attempts along these lines. An important aspect of intertemporal models that are based on Markov decision processes is that there exist powerful econometric techniques for structural estimation of the underlying parameters that describe the preferences and beliefs of economic agents. Such structural methods allow to derive valid out-of-sample forecasts and policy simulations because they are not subject to the *Lucas critique*. Ultimately, the usefulness of any MDP model has to be assessed by its empirical performance, and in this study, the application chosen was that of firm investment in the presence of financial constraints.

An application to joint investment and exit decisions

The theoretical framework of discrete Markov decision processes was applied in an empirical study of firms' investment decisions in the presence of financial constraints. The empirical results reported in Chapter 4 confirm that firm-level financial status has effects on plant-level investment and exit decisions. This result was obtained using a new measure of the firm's financial status which reflects more information than simple sample-split approaches. It was obtained both with reduced-form and structural dynamic discrete-choice models of firm behavior that account for endogenous exit decisions, a problem usually ignored in similar studies.

Also, this empirical application illustrates the fact that structural models allow for policy simulations that could not be performed using reduced-form methods. Here, the entire stochastic process of state and decision variables was simulated for an alternative policy (an environment without any financial constraints) and compared with the observed real-world data. This simulation exercise illustrates how plant growth and exit, and hence the evolution of the entire plant size distribution over time, are affected by financial constraints.

As discussed before, the model presented here surely has its limitations, the most serious of which is the exogeneity assumption imposed on the firm's financial situation in the empirical plant-level investment/exit model. Given the lack of more detailed data on the within-firm allocation of funds, and given the econometric techniques for intertemporal optimization models currently available, this was the only way to make the model operational. Hence, this application should be seen as a first step in this direction, showing that in principle, such an approach is practicable. In a more general model, one might wish to allow for a variety of more realistic features:

- a richer decision space, with more choice variables that are available to the firm and a finer discretization of the continuous choice variable, investment;
- more state variables with a finer discretization;
- more general forms of state transition dynamics (in particular, an endogenous financial status variable).

All of these extensions, however, will tremendously increase the dimension of the dynamic programming problem and its computational complexity. This is Bellman's famous "curse of dimensionality", an issue to which I return below.

An extension of the structural model in these directions, and constructing measures of firms' financial status for larger panels of firms, must be left to future research. It is my impression, however, that the latter task is more difficult. I would argue, hence, that the central problem of empirical tests of financial constraints is the proper measurement of firms' financial status rather than the formulation of the theoretical and empirical model.

The curse of dimensionality in practice

A note on the computational effort required to structurally estimate the kind of discrete dynamic decision processes considered in this study is in order here. The central issue is the dimensionality of the control-state space. Both the theoretical model and the existing software for estimation can be adapted to models with more state and control variables in a straightforward fashion. The binding restriction in this particular application is, however, the need to run the code on a UNIX workstation at the Center for Economic Studies – due to confidentiality of the Longitudinal Research Database, all computations had to be performed on site at the CES.

More generally, given the current levels of computing power, DDP models like those considered in this study reach the limit for the computational burden when estimation needs to be performed on standard workstations. Recall that the computational complexity of these DDP models is dominated by the number of state variables (and the number of discrete cells used to approximate continuous state variables). In addition to pure CPU speed, a major problem is that the size of the state transition matrix is restricted by the size of available core memory (as time-consuming swapping to virtual memory should be avoided).

Models which are more computationally burdensome in these terms require either more sophisticated estimation algorithms that might become available in the near future (such as randomized versions of the NFXP algorithm proposed by Rust (1997)), or the use of more powerful computer equipment. A particularly promising route is the use of massively parallel computation routines available on modern multi-processor supercomputers (or, using hardware-independent "remote procedure calls", on networks of smaller workstations) for performing operations on the state transition matrix, which is the computationally most demanding part of solving and structurally estimating a dynamic programming model.

In order to adjust the computational burden to these hardware restrictions, I chose the number of cells used in the discretization of the continuous state variables to allow overnight runs in actual estimation.[68] In the case of the investment/exit model presented in this study, even adding another discrete decision variable or a finer discretization of the state space would have rendered estimation virtually impossible on the workstations available for this project. The fact that some model spec-

[68] Note that for developing and testing the contraction algorithm that forms the inner loop of the nested fixed-point algorithm, I used a much finer grid; these tests confirmed that the coarse discretization version used at the CES still provides valid approximations to the value function.

ifications which are interesting from a theoretical viewpoint cannot be estimated due to hardware restrictions is certainly a serious restriction in empirical work, but given technical progress both in hardware speed and algorithm design, such restrictions are likely to be removed in the years to come.

List of figures

List of tables

Bibliography

Abel, A. B. (1980): Empirical investment equations: An integrative framework. *Carnegie-Rochester Conference Series on Public Policy*, 12, 39–91.

Abel, A. B. and O. J. Blanchard (1986): The present value of profits and cyclical movements in investment. *Econometrica*, 54, 249–273.

Abel, A. B., A. K. Dixit, J. C. Eberly, and R. S. Pindyck (1996): Options, the value of capital, and investment. *Quarterly Journal of Economics*, 111(3), 753–777.

Abowd, J. M., B. Crépon, F. Kramarz, and A. Trognon (1995): A la recherche des moments perdus: Covariance models for unbalanced panels with endogenous death. NBER Technical Working Paper No. 180.

An, M. Y. (1995): Econometric analysis of sequential discrete choice models. Working Paper No. 95-55, Department of Economics, Duke University.

Anderson, E. W., L. P. Hansen, E. McGrattan, and T. J. Sargent (1996): Mechanics of forming and estimating dynamic linear economies. In H. M. Amman, D. A. Kendrick, and J. Rust (Eds.), *Handbook of Computational Economics*, Volume 1, 171–252. Amsterdam: Elsevier.

Asplund, M. (1995): What fraction of a capital investment is sunk cost? Stockholm School of Economics Working Paper No. 68.

Baily, M. N., C. Hulten, and D. Campbell (1992): Productivity dynamics in manufacturing plants. *Brookings Papers on Economic Activity – Microeconomics*, 187–267.

Bain, J. (1956): *Barriers to New Competition.* Cambridge, MA: Harvard University Press.

Bartelsman, E. J. and W. B. Gray (1994): NBER Manufacturing Productivity Database. Unpublished manuscript, National Bureau of Economic Research.

Bellman, R. (1957): *Dynamic Programming.* Princeton, NJ: Princeton University Press.

Benitez-Silva, H., M. Buchinsky, H.-M. Chan, J. Rust, and S. Sheidvasser (1998): An empirical analysis of the Social Security disability application, appeal, and award process. Unpublished manuscript, Yale University.

Benveniste, L. M. and J. A. Scheinkman (1979): On the differentiability of the value function in dynamic models of economics. *Econometrica*, 47, 727–732.

Berger, A. N. and G. F. Udell (1992): Some evidence on the empirical significance of credit rationing. *Journal of Political Economy*, 100(5), 1047–1077.

Berkovec, J. and S. Stern (1991): Job exit behavior of older men. *Econometrica*, 59(1), 189–210.

Bernanke, B. S. and M. Gertler (1995): Inside the black box: The credit channel of monetary policy transmission. *Journal of Economic Perspectives*, 9(4), 27–48.

Bernanke, B. S., M. Gertler, and S. Gilchrist (1996): The financial accelerator and the flight to quality. *Review of Economics and Statistics*, 78(1), 1–15.

Berndt, E. R., B. H. Hall, R. E. Hall, and J. A. Hausman (1974): Estimation and inference in nonlinear structural models. *Annals of Economic and Social Measurement*, 3, 653–665.

Berry, S. T. (1992): Estimation of a model of entry in the airline industry. *Econometrica*, 60(4), 889–917.

Bertola, G. and R. J. Caballero (1990): Kinked adjustment costs and aggregate dynamics. In O. J. Blanchard and S. Fischer (Eds.), *NBER Macroeconomics Annual*, Volume 5, 237–288. Cambridge, MA: MIT Press.

Bertola, G. and R. J. Caballero (1994): Irreversibility and aggregate investment. *Review of Economic Studies*, 61, 223–246.

Bertsekas, D. P. (1976): *Dynamic Programming and Stochastic Control.* New York, San Francisco and London: Academic Press.

Bertsekas, D. P. (1995): *Dynamic Programming and Optimal Control, Vols. 1 & 2.* Belmont, MA: Athena Scientific.

Bester, H. and M. Hellwig (1987): Moral hazard and equilibrium credit rationing: An overview of the issues. In G. Bamberg and K. Spremann (Eds.), *Agency Theory, Information and Incentives.* Heidelberg: Springer.

Bhattacharya, R. N. and M. Majumdar (1989): Controlled semi-Markov models: The discounted case. *Journal of Statistical Planning and Inference*, 21, 365–381.

Blackwell, D. (1965): Discounted dynamic programming. *Annals of Mathematical Statistics*, 36, 226–235.

Blanchard, O. J. and S. Fischer (1989): *Lectures on Macroeconomics*. Cambridge, MA: MIT Press.

Blanchard, O. J., F. Lopez-de-Silanes, and A. Shleifer (1994): What do firms do with cash windfalls? *Journal of Financial Economics*, 36, 337 –360.

Blau, D. (1994): A structural model of retirement-related labor market dynamics. *Econometrica*, 62(1), 117–156.

Blundell, R., S. Bond, and C. Meghir (1996): Econometric models of company investment. In L. Mátyás and P. Sevestre (Eds.), *The Econometrics of Panel Data: A Handbook of the Theory with Applications. Second Revised Edition*, 685–710. Amsterdam: Kluwer.

Bond, S. and C. Meghir (1994): Dynamic investment models and firms' financial policy. *Review of Economic Studies*, 61, 197–222.

Börsch-Supan, A. and V. A. Hajivassiliou (1993): Smooth unbiased multivariate probability simulators for maximum likelihood estimation of limited dependent variable models. *Journal of Econometrics*, 58, 347–368.

Burtless, G. (1989): Comment on Rust: "A dynamic programming model of retirement behavior". In D. A. Wise (Ed.), *The Economics of Aging*, 398 –403. Chicago, IL, and London: University of Chicago Press.

Caballero, R. J. and E. M. R. A. Engel (1994): Explaining investment dynamics in U.S. manufacturing: A generalized (S,s) approach. NBER Working Paper No. 4887.

Caballero, R. J., E. M. R. A. Engel, and J. C. Haltiwanger (1997): Aggregate employment dynamics: Building from microeconomic evidence. *American Economic Review*, 87(1), 115–137.

Caballero, R. J. and M. L. Hammour (1994): The cleansing effect of recessions. *American Economic Review*, 84(5), 1350–1368.

Caballero, R. J. and J. V. Leahy (1996): Fixed costs: The demise of marginal q. NBER Working Paper No. 5508.

Caballero, R. J. and R. S. Pindyck (1996): Uncertainty, investment, and industry evolution. *International Economic Review*, 37(3), 641–662.

Calomiris, C. W. and C. P. Himmelberg (1998): Investment banking costs as a measure of the cost of access to external finance. Unpublished manuscript, Columbia University.

Calomiris, C. W., A. Orphanides, and S. A. Sharpe (1994): Leverage as a state variable for employment, inventory accumulation, and fixed investment. NBER Working Paper No. 4800.

Camerer, C. (1995): Individual decision making. In J. H. Kagel and A. E. Roth (Eds.), *Handbook of Experimental Economics*, 587–703. Princeton, NJ: Princeton University Press.

Carpenter, R. E., S. M. Fazzari, and B. C. Petersen (1994): Inventory investment, internal-finance fluctuations, and the business cycle. *Brookings Papers on Economic Activity*, No. 2, 75–138.

Center for Economic Studies (1992): Longitudinal Research Database: Technical Documentation Manual. Unpublished manuscript, U.S. Bureau of the Census, Washington, D.C.

Chirinko, R. S. (1993): Business fixed investment spending: Modeling strategies, empirical results, and policy implications. *Journal of Economic Literature*, 31, 1875–1911.

Chirinko, R. S. and H. Schaller (1995): Why does liquidity matter in investment equations? *Journal of Money, Credit and Banking*, 25(2), 527–548.

Christiano, L. J. and J. D. M. Fisher (1997): Algorithms for solving dynamic models with occasionally binding constraints. Working Paper No. 97-15, Research Department, Federal Reserve Bank of Chicago.

Coleman, W. J. (1991): Equilibrium in a production economy with income tax. *Econometrica*, 59(4), 1091–1104.

Cooper, R., J. C. Haltiwanger, and L. Power (1995): Machine replacement and the business cycle: Lumps and bumps. NBER Working Paper No. 5260.

Corres, S., V. A. Hajivassiliou, and Y. M. Ioannides (1997): An empirical investigation of the dynamics of qualitative decisions of firms. Unpublished manuscript, London School of Economics and Virginia Polytechnic Institute and State University.

Corres, S. and Y. M. Ioannides (1994): Endogenous attrition of firms: An investigation with Compustat data. Unpublished manuscript, Virginia Polytechnic.

Das, S. (1992): A micro-econometric model of capital utilization and retirement: The case of the U.S. cement industry. *Review of Economic Studies*, 59, 277–297.

Das, S. and S. P. Das (1996): Dynamics of entry and exit of firms in the presence of entry adjustment costs. *International Journal of Industrial Organization*, 15, 217–241.

Davis, S. J., J. C. Haltiwanger, and S. Schuh (1996): *Job Creation and Destruction.* Cambridge, MA: MIT Press.

de Meza, D. and D. C. Webb (1987): Too much investment: A problem of asymmetric information. *Quarterly Journal of Economics*, 102, 281–292.

Deaton, A. (1991): Saving and liquidity constraints. *Econometrica*, 59(5), 1221–1248.

Diamond, D. W. (1984): Financial intermediation and delegated monitoring. *Review of Economic Studies*, 51, 393–414.

Dixit, A. K. (1989): Entry and exit decisions under uncertainty. *Journal of Political Economy*, 97, 620–638.

Dixit, A. K. and R. S. Pindyck (1994): *Investment under Uncertainty.* Princeton, NJ: Princeton University Press.

Doms, M., T. Dunne, and M. J. Roberts (1995): The role of technology use in the survival and growth of manufacturing plants. *International Journal of Industrial Organization*, 13(4), 523–542.

Dunne, T., J. C. Haltiwanger, and K. R. Troske (1997): Technology and jobs: Secular changes and cyclical dynamics. *Carnegie-Rochester Conference Series on Public Policy*, 46(1), 107–178.

Dunne, T., M. J. Roberts, and L. Samuelson (1988): Patterns of firm entry and exit in U.S. manufacturing industries. *Rand Journal of Economics*, 19(4), 495–515.

Dunne, T., M. J. Roberts, and L. Samuelson (1989): The growth and failure of U.S. manufacturing plants. *Quarterly Journal of Economics*, 104(4), 671–698.

Eberly, J. C. (1993): Comment on Pindyck and Solimano: "Economic instability and aggregate investment". In O. Blanchard and S. Fischer (Eds.), *NBER Macroeconomics Annual*, Volume 8, 303–312. Cambridge, MA: MIT Press.

Eckstein, Z. and K. I. Wolpin (1989): Dynamic labour force participation of married women and endogenous work experience. *Review of Economic Studies*, 56, 375–390.

Eichenbaum, M. (1994): Comment on Kashyap and Stein: "Monetary policy and bank lending". In N. G. Mankiw (Ed.), *Monetary Policy*, 256–257. Chicago and London: University of Chicago Press.

Eisner, R. and R. H. Strotz (1963): Determinants of business investment. In D. B. Suits (Ed.), *Impacts of Monetary Policy*, 59–233. Englewood Cliffs, NJ: Prentice-Hall.

Ericson, R. and A. Pakes (1995): Markov-perfect industry dynamics: A framework for empirical work. *Review of Economic Studies*, 62(1), 53–82.

Fair, R. C. (1996): Computational methods for macroeconomic models. In H. M. Amman, D. A. Kendrick, and J. Rust (Eds.), *Handbook of Computational Economics*, Volume 1, 143–169. Amsterdam: Elsevier.

Fair, R. C. and J. B. Taylor (1983): Solution and maximum likelihood estimation of dynamic nonlinear rational expectations models. *Econometrica*, 51, 1269–1286.

Fazzari, S. M., R. G. Hubbard, and B. C. Petersen (1988): Financing constraints and corporate investment. *Brookings Papers on Economic Activity*, No. 1, 141–195.

Fazzari, S. M., R. G. Hubbard, and B. C. Petersen (1996): Financing constraints and corporate investment: Response to Kaplan and Zingales. NBER Working Paper No. 5462.

Fisher, I. (1933): The debt-deflation theory of great depressions. *Econometrica*, 1(5), 337–357.

Friedman, M. (1953): *Essays in Positive Economics*. Chicago, IL, and London: Cambridge University Press.

Fudenberg, D. and J. Tirole (1986): A "signal-jamming" theory of predation. *Rand Journal of Economics*, 17(3), 366–376.

Fuhrer, J. C., G. R. Moore, and S. D. Schuh (1995): Estimating the linear-quadratic inventory model: Maximum likelihood versus generalized method of moments. *Journal of Monetary Economics*, 35, 115–157.

Gale, D. and M. Hellwig (1985): Incentive compatible debt contracts I: The one period problem. *Review of Economic Studies*, 52, 647–664.

Geroski, P. A. (1991): *Market Dynamics and Entry*. London: Basil Blackwell.

Gertler, M. (1992): Financial capacity and output fluctuations in an economy with multi-period financial relationships. *Review of Economic Studies*, 59, 455–472.

Gertler, M. and S. Gilchrist (1994): Monetary policy, business cycles and the behavior of small manufacturing firms. *Quarterly Journal of Economics*, 109(2), 309–340.

Gertner, R. H., D. S. Scharfstein, and J. C. Stein (1994): Internal vs. external capital markets. *Quarterly Journal of Economics*, 109(4), 1211–1230.

Geweke, J. (1996): Monte Carlo simulation and numerical integration. In H. M. Amman, D. A. Kendrick, and J. Rust (Eds.), *Handbook of Computational Economics*, Volume 1, 731–800. Amsterdam: Elsevier.

Gilchrist, S. and C. P. Himmelberg (1995): Evidence on the role of cash flow on investment. *Journal of Monetary Economics*, 36, 541–572.

Gilchrist, S. and C. P. Himmelberg (1998): Investment, fundamentals and finance. Forthcoming, *NBER Macroeconomics Annual*.

Gould, J. P. (1968): Adjustment costs in the theory of investment of the firm. *Review of Economic Studies*, 35, 47–56.

Greenwald, B. C. and J. E. Stiglitz (1993): Financial market imperfections and business cycles. *Quarterly Journal of Economics*, 108, 77–114.

Hajivassiliou, V. A. (1993): Simulation estimation methods for limited dependent variable models. In G. S. Maddala, C. R. Rao, and H. D. Vinod (Eds.), *Handbook of Statistics*, Volume 11, 519–543. Amsterdam: Elsevier.

Hajivassiliou, V. A. and Y. M. Ioannides (1991): Switching regression models of the Euler equation: Consumption, labor supply, and liquidity constraints. Cowles Foundation Discussion Paper, Yale University.

Hajivassiliou, V. A. and Y. M. Ioannides (1994): Unemployment and liquidity constraints. Unpublished manuscript.

Hajivassiliou, V. A. and Y. M. Ioannides (1996): Duality and liquidity constraints under uncertainty. *Journal of Economic Dynamics and Control*, 20(6-7), 1177–1192.

Hall, A. (1993): Some aspects of generalized method of moments estimation. In G. S. Maddala, C. R. Rao, and H. D. Vinod (Eds.), *Handbook of Statistics*, Volume 11, 393–417. Amsterdam: Elsevier.

Hall, B. H. (1987): The relationship between firm size and firm growth in the U.S. manufacturing sector. *Journal of Industrial Economics*, 35(4), 583 –606.

Hall, B. H. (1990): The Manufacturing Sector Master File: 1959-1987. NBER Working Paper No. 3366.

Hamermesh, D. S. and G. A. Pfann (1996): Adjustment costs in factor demand. *Journal of Economic Literature*, 34(3), 1264–1292.

Hansen, L. P. (1982): Large sample properties of generalized method of moments estimators. *Econometrica*, 50(4), 1029–1054.

Hansen, L. P. and T. J. Sargent (1980): Formulating and estimating dynamic linear rational expectations models. *Journal of Economic Dynamics and Control*, 2(1), 7–46.

Hansen, L. P. and T. J. Sargent (1981): Linear rational expectations models for dynamically interrelated variables. In R. E. Lucas and T. J. Sargent (Eds.), *Rational Expectations and Econometric Practice*, 127–156. Minneapolis, MN: University of Minnesota Press.

Hansen, L. P. and K. J. Singleton (1982): Generalized instrumental variables estimation of nonlinear rational expectation models. *Econometrica*, 50(5), 1269–1286.

Harris, M. and A. Raviv (1996): The capital budgeting process: Incentives and information. *Journal of Finance*, 51(4), 1139–1174.

Hartley, P. R. (1996): Value function approximation in the presence of uncertainty and inequality constraints: An application to the demand for credit cards. *Journal of Economic Dynamics and Control*, 20, 63–92.

Hayashi, F. (1982): Tobin's marginal q and average q: A neoclassical interpretation. *Econometrica*, 50(1), 213–224.

Heckman, J. J. (1976): The common structure of statistical models of truncation, sample selection, and limited dependent variables and a simple estimator for such models. *Annals of Economic and Social Measurement*, 5(4), 475–492.

Heckman, J. J. (1979): Sample selection bias as a specification error. *Econometrica*, 47(1), 153–161.

Hellwig, M. (1990): Banking, financial intermediation and corporate finance. In A. Giovannini and C. Mayer (Eds.), *European Financial Integration*, 35–63. Cambridge, England: Cambridge University Press.

Himmelberg, C. P. and B. C. Petersen (1994): R&D and internal finance: A panel study of small firms in high-tech industries. *Review of Economics and Statistics*, 76(1), 38–51.

Holtz-Eakin, D., D. Joulfaian, and H. S. Rosen (1994): Sticking it out: Entrepreneurial survival and liquidity constraints. *Journal of Political Economy*, 102(1), 53–75.

Hopenhayn, H. A. (1992): Entry, exit, and firm dynamics in long run equilibrium. *Econometrica*, 60(5), 1127–1150.

Hotz, V. J. and R. A. Miller (1993): Conditional choice probabilities and the estimation of dynamic models. *Review of Economic Studies*, 60, 497–529.

Hotz, V. J., R. A. Miller, S. Sanders, and J. Smith (1994): A simulation estimator for dynamic models of discrete choice. *Review of Economic Studies*, 61, 265–289.

Hubbard, R. G. (1994): Is there a 'credit channel' for monetary policy? NBER Working Paper No. 4977.

Hubbard, R. G. (1998): Capital-market imperfections and investment. *Journal of Economic Literature*, 36(1), 193–225.

Hubbard, R. G., A. K. Kashyap, and T. M. Whited (1995): Internal finance and firm investment. *Journal of Money, Credit and Banking*, 27(3), 683–701.

Hulten, C. R. and F. C. Wykoff (1981): The measurement of economic depreciation. In C. R. Hulten (Ed.), *Depreciation, Inflation, and the Taxation of Income from Capital.* Washington, D.C.: Urban Institute.

İmrohoroğlu, A. (1989): Cost of business cycles with indivisibilities and liquidity constraints. *Journal of Political Economy*, 97(6), 1364–1383.

Isgut, A. E. (1997): Irreversible investment: Empirical evidence from Colombian microdata. Unpublished manuscript, Wesleyan University.

Jaffee, D. and J. E. Stiglitz (1990): Credit rationing. In B. J. Friedman and F. Hahn (Eds.), *Handbook of Monetary Economics*, Volume 2, 837–888. Amsterdam: North-Holland.

Japelli, T., J.-S. Pischke, and N. S. Souleles (1997): Testing for liquidity constraints in Euler equations with complementary data sources. Rodney L. White Center for Financial Research Working Paper No. 10-97, The Wharton School, University of Pennsylvania.

Jensen, M. C. (1986): Agency costs of free cash flow, corporate finance, and takeovers. *American Economic Review, Papers & Proceedings*, 76(2), 323–329.

Jensen, M. C. (1993): The modern industrial revolution, exit, and the failure of internal control systems. *Journal of Finance*, 48(3), 831–880.

Jorgenson, D. W. (1963): Capital theory and investment behaviour. *American Economic Review, Papers & Proceedings*, 53(2), 247–259.

Jorgenson, D. W. (1967): The theory of investment behavior. In R. Ferber (Ed.), *Determinants of Investment Behavior*, 129–155. New York: National Bureau of Economic Research.

Jorgenson, D. W. (1971): Econometric studies of investment behavior: A survey. *Journal of Economic Literature*, 9, 1111–1147.

Jovanovic, B. (1982): Selection and the evolution of industry. *Econometrica*, 50(3), 649–670.

Judd, K. L. (1994): Comments on Marcet, Rust and Pakes. In C. A. Sims (Ed.), *Advances in Econometrics: Sixth World Congress*, Volume 2, 261–274. Cambridge, England: Cambridge University Press.

Judd, K. L. (1996): Approximation, pertubation, and projection methods in economic analysis. In H. M. Amman, D. A. Kendrick, and J. Rust (Eds.), *Handbook of Computational Economics*, Volume 1, 509–585. Amsterdam: Elsevier.

Kaplan, S. N. and L. Zingales (1995): Do financing constraints explain why investment is correlated with cash flow? NBER Working Paper No. 5267.

Kaplan, S. N. and L. Zingales (1997): Do investment-cash flow sensitivities provide useful measures of financing constraints? *Quarterly Journal of Economics*, 112(1), 169–215.

Kashyap, A. K., O. A. Lamont, and J. C. Stein (1994): Credit conditions and the cyclical behavior of inventories. *Quarterly Journal of Economics*, 109(3), 565–592.

Kashyap, A. K. and J. C. Stein (1994): Monetary policy and bank lending. In N. G. Mankiw (Ed.), *Monetary Policy*, 221–256. Chicago and London: University of Chicago Press.

Keane, M. P. and K. I. Wolpin (1997): Introduction to the *JBES* special issue on structural estimation in applied microeconomics. *Journal of Business and Economics Statistics*, 15(2), 111–114.

Kovenock, D. and G. M. Phillips (1995): Capital structure and product market rivalry: How do we reconcile theory and evidence? *American Economic Review, Papers & Proceedings*, 85(2), 403–408.

Kovenock, D. and G. M. Phillips (1997): Capital structure and product market behavior: An examination of plant exit and investment decisions. *Review of Financial Studies*, 10(3), 767–803.

Lambson, V. E. (1991): Industry evolution with sunk costs and uncertain market conditions. *International Journal of Industrial Organization*, 9, 171 –196.

Lamont, O. (1997): Cash flow and investment: Evidence from internal capital markets. *Journal of Finance*, 52(1), 83–109.

Leahy, J. V. and T. M. Whited (1996): The effect of uncertainty on investment: Some stylized facts. *Journal of Money, Credit and Banking*, 28(1), 64–83.

Lichtenberg, F. R. and D. Siegel (1991): The impact of R&D investment on productivity: New evidence using linked R&D-LRD data. *Economic Enquiry*, 29(2), 203–229.

Lucas, D. J. and R. L. McDonald (1992): Bank financing and investment decisions with asymmetric information about loan quality. *Rand Journal of Economics*, 23(1), 86–105.

Lucas, R. E. (1976): Econometric policy evaluation: A critique. *Carnegie-Rochester Conference Series on Public Policy*, 1, 19–46.

Lucas, R. E. and E. C. Prescott (1971): Investment under uncertainty. *Econometrica*, 39, 659–681.

Lumsdaine, R. L., J. H. Stock, and D. A. Wise (1992): Three models of retirement: Computational complexity versus predictive validity. In D. A. Wise (Ed.), *Topics in the Economics of Aging*, 21–57. Chicago and London: University of Chicago Press.

Maksimovic, V. (1996): Financial structure and product market competition. In R. A. Jarrow, V. Maksimovic, and W. T. Ziemba (Eds.), *Handbooks in Operations Research and Management Science*, Volume 9: Finance, 887 –920. Amsterdam et al.: Elsevier.

Mankiw, N. G. (1986): The allocation of credit and financial collapse. *Quarterly Journal of Economics*, 101, 455–470.

Marcet, A. (1994): Simulation analysis of dynamic stochastic models: Applications to theory and estimation. In C. A. Sims (Ed.), *Advances in Econometrics, Sixth World Congress*, Volume Volume 2, 81–118. Cambridge, England: Cambridge University Press.

Marschak, J. (1952): Economic measurements for policy and prediction. In W. C. Hood and T. C. Koopmans (Eds.), *Studies in Econometric Method*, 1–26. New York: Wiley.

Matsusaka, J. G. and V. Nanda (1996): Internal capital markets and corporate refocusing. Unpublished manuscript, School of Business Administration, University of Michigan.

McDonald, R. L. and D. R. Siegel (1986): The value of waiting to invest. *Quarterly Journal of Economics*, 101, 707–727.

McFadden, D. F. (1981): Econometric models of probabilistic choice. In C. F. Manski and D. F. McFadden (Eds.), *Structural Analysis of Discrete Data with Econometric Applications*, 198–272. Cambridge, MA: MIT Press.

McFadden, D. F. (1989): A method of simulated moments for estimation of discrete choice response models without numerical integration. *Econometrica*, 57(5), 995–1026.

McGrattan, E. R. (1997): Application of weighted residual methods to dynamic economic problems. Federal Reserve Bank of Minneapolis, Research Department Staff Report 232.

McGuckin, R. H. (1995): Establishment microdata in economic research and policy analysis: Looking beyond the aggregates. *Journal of Business Economics and Statistics*, 13(1), 121–126.

McGuckin, R. H. and S. V. Nguyen (1995): On productivity and plant ownership change: New evidence from the Longitudinal Research Database. *Rand Journal of Economics*, 26(2), 257–276.

McGuckin, R. H. and G. A. Pascoe (1988): The Longitudinal Research Database: Status and research possibilities. *Survey of Current Business*, November, 30–37.

Meltzer, A. H. (1995): Monetary, credit (and other) transmission processes: A Monetarist perspective. *Journal of Economic Perspectives*, 9(4), 49–72.

Meyer, B. D. (1995): Natural and quasi-experiments in economics. *Journal of Business and Economics Statistics*, 13(2), 151–161.

Milne, A. and D. Robertson (1996): Firm behavior under the threat of liquidation. *Journal of Economic Dynamics and Control*, 20, 1427–1449.

Mishkin, F. S. (1995): Symposium on the monetary transmission mechanism. *Journal of Economic Perspectives*, 9(4), 3–10.

Modigliani, F. and M. H. Miller (1958): The cost of capital, corporation finance, and the theory of investment. *American Economic Review*, 48(3), 261–297.

Montgomery, C. A. (1994): Corporate diversification. *Journal of Economic Perspectives*, 8(3), 163–178.

Montgomery, M. R. (1991): Migration and job search in Malaysia. Unpublished manuscript, SUNY at Stony Brook.

Myers, S. C. and N. Majluf (1984): Corporate financing and investment decisions when firms have information that investors do not have. *Journal of Financial Economics*, 13(2), 187–221.

Naylor, A. W. and G. R. Sell (1982): *Linear Operator Theory in Engineering and Science*. New York, Heidelberg and Berlin: Springer-Verlag.

Nickell, S. J. (1978): *The Investment Decisions of Firms*. Cambridge, UK: Cambridge University Press.

Obstfeld, M. and K. Rogoff (1995): The mirage of fixed exchange rates. *Journal of Economic Perspectives*, 9(4), 73–96.

Ofek, E. (1993): Capital structure and firm response to poor performance: An empirical analysis. *Journal of Financial Economics*, 34, 3–30.

Ogaki, M. (1993): Generalized Method of Moments: Econometric applications. In G. S. Maddala, C. R. Rao, and H. D. Vinod (Eds.), *Handbook of Statistics*, Volume 11, 455–488. Amsterdam: Elsevier.

Oliner, S. D. and G. D. Rudebusch (1996): Is there a broad credit channel for monetary policy? *Federal Reserve Bank of San Francisco Economic Review*, No. 1, 3–13.

Oliner, S. D., G. D. Rudebusch, and D. Sichel (1995): New and old models of business investment: A comparison of forecasting performance. *Journal of Money, Credit and Banking*, 27(3), 806–826.

Olley, G. S. and A. Pakes (1996): The dynamics of productivity in the telecommunications equipment industry. *Econometrica*, 64(6), 1263–1297.

Pakes, A. (1986): Patents as options: Some estimates of the value of holding European patent stocks. *Econometrica*, 54(4), 755–784.

Pakes, A. (1994): Dynamic structural models, problems and prospects: Mixed continuous discrete controls and market interactions. In C. A. Sims (Ed.), *Advances in Econometrics: Sixth World Congress*, Volume 2, 171–274. Cambridge, England: Cambridge University Press.

Pakes, A. and R. Ericson (1990): Empirical implications of alternative models of firm dynamics. Unpublished manuscript, Yale University.

Pakes, A., G. Gowrisankaran, and P. McGuire (1993): Implementing the Pakes-McGuire algorithm for computing Markov-perfect equilibria in Gauss. Unpublished manuscript, Yale University.

Pakes, A. and P. McGuire (1994): Computing Markov-perfect Nash equilibria: Numerical implications of a dynamic differentiated product model. *Rand Journal of Economics*, 25(4), 555–589.

Pakes, A. and P. McGuire (1995): Computing Markov-perfect Nash equilibria II: Approximations. Unpublished manuscript, Yale University.

Pakes, A. and P. McGuire (1996): Stochastic algorithms for dynamic models: Markov-perfect equilbrium and the "curse" of dimensionality. Unpublished manuscript, Yale University.

Pakes, A. and S. Olley (1995): A limit theorem for a smooth class of semiparametric estimators. *Journal of Econometrics*, 65, 295–332.

Pemberton, J. (1993): Attainable non-optimality or unattainable optimality: A new approach to stochastic life cycle problems. *Economic Journal*, 103, 1–20.

Pindyck, R. S. and A. Solimano (1993): Economic instability and aggregate investment. In O. J. Blanchard and S. Fischer (Eds.), *NBER Macroeconomics Annual*, Volume 8, 259–303. Cambridge, MA: MIT Press.

Pudney, S. (1989): *Modelling Individual Choice.* Oxford, England and New York, NY: Basil Blackwell.

Puterman, M. L. (1994): *Markov Decision Processes.* New York: Wiley.

Ravenscroft, D. J. and F. M. Scherer (1987): *Mergers, Sell-Offs, and Economics Efficiency.* Washington, D.C.: Brookings Institution.

Rothwell, G. and J. Rust (1995): A dynamic programming model of U.S. nuclear power plant operations. Unpublished manuscript, Stanford University and University of Wisconsin–Madison.

Rothwell, G. and J. Rust (1997): On the optimal lifetime of nuclear power plants. *Journal of Business and Economics Statistics*, 15(2), 195–208.

Rust, J. (1987): Optimal replacement of GMC bus engines: An empirical model of Harold Zurcher. *Econometrica*, 55(5), 999–1033.

Rust, J. (1988): Maximum likelihood estimation of discrete control processes. *SIAM Journal on Control and Optimization*, 26(5), 1006–1024.

Rust, J. (1989): A dynamic programming model of retirement behavior. In D. A. Wise (Ed.), *The Economics of Aging*, 359–398. Chicago, IL, and London: University of Chicago Press.

Rust, J. (1990): Behavior of male workers at the end of the life cycle: An empirical analysis of states and controls. In D. A. Wise (Ed.), *Issues in the Economics of Aging*, 317–379. Chicago, IL, and London: University of Chicago Press.

Rust, J. (1992): A dynamic programming model of retirement behavior. In K. R. Billingsley, H. U. Brown, and E. Derohanes (Eds.), *Computer Assisted Modeling on the IBM 3090*, Volume 2, 887–912. Atlanta, GA: Baldwin Press.

Rust, J. (1994a): Do people behave according to Bellman's principle of optimality? Unpublished manuscript, University of Wisconsin–Madison.

Rust, J. (1994b): Estimation of dynamic structural models, problems and prospects: Discrete decision processes. In C. A. Sims (Ed.), *Advances in Econometrics: Sixth World Congress*, Volume 2, 119–170. Cambridge, England: Cambridge University Press.

Rust, J. (1994c): Numerical dynamic programming in economics. Unpublished draft for the *Handbook of Computational Economics*, University of Wisconsin–Madison.

Rust, J. (1994d): Structural estimation of Markov decision processes. In R. F. Engle and D. L. McFadden (Eds.), *Handbook of Econometrics*, Volume 4, 3081–3143. Amsterdam: Elsevier (North-Holland).

Rust, J. (1995): Nested Fixed-Point Algorithm Documentation Manual, Version 5. Mimeograph, University of Wisconsin–Madison.

Rust, J. (1996): Numerical dynamic programming in economics. In H. M. Amman, D. A. Kendrick, and J. Rust (Eds.), *Handbook of Computational Economics*, Volume 1, 619–729. Amsterdam: Elsevier.

Rust, J. (1997): Using randomization to break the curse of dimensionality. *Econometrica*, 65(3), 487–516.

Rust, J. and C. Phelan (1997): How Social Security and Medicare affect retirement behavior in a world of incomplete markets. *Econometrica*, 65(4), 781–831.

Rust, J. and G. Rothwell (1995): Optimal response to a shift in regulatory regime: The case of the U.S. nuclear power industry. *Journal of Applied Econometrics*, 10, S75–S118.

Sargent, T. J. (1976): Estimation of dynamic labor demand schedules under rational expectations. *Journal of Political Economy*, 86(6), 1009–1044.

Sargent, T. J. (1987a): *Dynamic Macroeconomic Theory*. Cambridge, MA, and London: Harvard University Press.

Sargent, T. J. (1987b): *Macroeconomic Theory*. 2nd Edition. San Diego, CA: Academic Press.

Sargent, T. J. (1996): Recursive macroeconomic theory. Unpublished manuscript, University of Chicago.

Shin, H.-H. and R. M. Stulz (1996): Is the internal capital market efficient? Unpublished manuscript, University of Oregon and Ohio State University.

Shleifer, A. and L. H. Summers (1988): Breach of trust in hostile takeovers. In A. J. Auerbach (Ed.), *Corporate Takeovers: Causes and Consequences*, 33–56. Chicago, IL, and London: University of Chicago Press.

Shleifer, A. and R. W. Vishny (1992): Liquidation values and debt capacity: A market equilibrium approach. *Journal of Finance*, 47(4), 1343 –1366.

Shleifer, A. and R. W. Vishny (1997): A survey of corporate governance. *Journal of Finance*, 52(2), 737–783.

Siegfried, J. J. and L. B. Evans (1994): Empirical studies of entry and exit: A survey of the evidence. *Review of Industrial Organization*, 9, 121–155.

Silverman, B. W. (1986): *Density Estimation for Statistics and Data Analysis.* London and New York: Chapman and Hall.

Siow, A. and X. Zhu (1997): The creation of plants and firms. *Journal of Economic Dynamics and Control*, 22, 141–178.

Stein, J. C. (1997): Internal capital markets and the competition for corporate resources. *Journal of Finance*, 52(1), 111–133.

Stern, S. (1997): Simulation-based estimation. *Journal of Economic Literature*, 35(4), 2006–2039.

Stiglitz, J. E. and A. Weiss (1981): Credit rationing in markets with imperfect information. *American Economic Review*, 71(3), 393–410.

Stiglitz, J. E. and A. Weiss (1987): Macroeconomic equilibrium and credit rationing. NBER Working Paper No. 2164.

Stokey, N. L. and R. E. Lucas (1989): *Recursive Methods in Economic Dynamics.* Cambridge, MA, and London: Harvard University Press.

Summers, L. H. (1981): Taxation and corporate investment: A q-theory approach. *Brookings Papers on Economic Activity*, No. 1.

Sylos-Labini, P. (1962): *Oligopoly and Technical Progress.* Cambridge, MA: Harvard University Press.

Taylor, J. B. (1995): The monetary transmission mechanism: An empirical framework. *Journal of Economic Perspectives*, 9(4), 11–26.

Treadway, A. B. (1969): On rational entrepreneurial behaviour and the demand for investment. *Review of Economic Studies*, 36, 227–239.

U.S. Bureau of Economic Analysis (1984): The input-output structure of the U.S. economy, 1977. *Survey of Current Business*, 65(5), 42–84.

U.S. Bureau of Labor Statistics (1983): *Trends in Multifactor Productivity, 1948-81.* BLS Bulletin 2178. Washington, D.C.: U.S. Government Printing Office.

Verbeek, M. and T. Nijman (1996): Incomplete panels and selection bias. In L. Mátyás and P. Sevestre (Eds.), *The Econometrics of Panel Data, Second Revised Edition*, 449–490. Dordrecht, Boston and London: Kluwer.

Whited, T. M. (1992): Debt, liquidity constraints, and corporate investment: Evidence from panel data. *Journal of Finance*, 47(4), 1425–1460.

Whited, T. M. (1994): Problems with identifying adjustment costs from regressions of investment on *q*. *Economics Letters*, 46, 339–344.

Williamson, O. E. (1975): *Markets and Hierarchies: Analysis and Antitrust Implications.* New York, NY: The Free Press.

Williamson, S. D. (1986): Costly monitoring, financial intermediation, and equilibrium rationing. *Journal of Monetary Economics*, 18, 159–179.

Witte, J. G. (1963): The microfoundations of the social investment function. *Journal of Political Economy*, 71(5), 441–456.

Wolpin, K. I. (1984): An estimable dynamic stochastic model of fertility and child mortality. *Journal of Political Economy*, 92(5), 852–874.

Wolpin, K. I. (1996): Public-policy uses of discrete-choice dynamic programming models. *American Economic Review, Papers & Proceedings*, 86(2), 427–432.

Zeldes, S. P. (1989): Consumption and liquidity constraints: An empirical investigation. *Journal of Political Economy*, 97(2), 305–346.

Contributions to Economics

Hagen Bobzin
Indivisibilities
1998. ISBN 3-7908-1123-8

Helmut Wagner (Ed.)
Current Issues in Monetary Economics
1998. ISBN 3-7908-1127-0

Peter Michaelis/Frank Stähler (Eds.)
Recent Policy Issues in Environmental and Resource Economics
1998. ISBN 3-7908-1137-8

Jessica de Wolff
The Political Economy of Fiscal Decisions
1998. ISBN 3-7908-1130-0

Georg Bol/Gholamreza Nakhaeizadeh/
Karl-Heinz Vollmer (Eds.)
Risk Measurements, Econometrics and Neural Networks
1998. ISBN 3-7908-1152-1